**Ernst A. Heiniger**

# Grand Canyon

Texts

**Joseph Wood Krutch †**
**Hans Boesch**
**William A. Weber**
**Heini Hediger**
**Jean Heiniger**

German texts translated by Ewald Osers

Robert B. Luce Co., Inc.
Washington—New York

Cartography, photolithography and printing:
Kümmerly and Frey, Graphical Institute, Berne/Switzerland
Color photographs: Nikon camera on Kodachrome film
Graphics: Ernst A. Heiniger, Zürich
Printed in Switzerland
Copyright © 1971 by Kümmerly and Frey, Geographical Publishers, Berne/Switzerland
ISBN 0-88331-074-0

Published in the United States 1975
Library of Congress Card Catalog Number 74-17517

The book includes:        a relief map of the U.S.A. — 1 : 13,000,000
two survey maps
an anaglyphic map
eight sketches and diagrams

# Contents

9   Dr. Joseph Wood Krutch †   Foreword

17   Dr. Hans Boesch   Geography, Geology, History

97   Dr. William A. Weber   Botany

161   Dr. Heini Hediger   Fauna

217   Jean Heiniger   A Year at the Grand Canyon

Commentary on Pictures

This book is dedicated to Walt Disney in remembrance of our great friendship, and with gratitude for it was Walt who introduced me to the beauties of the Grand Canyon.

E. S. Heinige

# Foreword

Grand Canyon was young—only a few million years old—when the first European came suddenly (as today's visitor still does) onto the edge of a vast abyss. His name was Cárdenas and he had been dispatched by the great conquistador Coronado with orders to scout out the region for signs of the Seven Golden Cities of Cibola—which of course did not exist.

Like "stout Cortez" in John Keat's poem, he must have looked into its depths "in wild surmise". But to him it was neither a sublime spectacle, a geological marvel, nor a biological unit ecologically fascinating. It was merely an unconquerable obstacle to a weary traveler which mocked him with a "thus far shalt thou go and no further".

In the pages which follow several experts will comment briefly on the geological and biological meaning of the Canyon. Perhaps this short introduction can do nothing more useful than to indicate the stages by which this unwelcomed sight was transformed into one of the most visited beauty spots of the world and recognized as what has been called the most revealing single page of earth's history anywhere laid open to be read by even the most casual amateur.

The other white men known to have seen the Canyon during the next three centuries could be counted on the fingers of one hand. And not until 1857 did the United States government think any of the Southwest sufficiently worth investigating to dispatch a certain Lieutenant Ives on an extensive reconnaissance of the regions around the lower reaches of the Canyon. His report included this significant statement: "Ours has been the first and will doubtless be the last party of whites to visit this profitless locality. It seems intended by nature that the Colorado River, along the greater portion of its lonely and majestic way, shall be forever unvisited and undisturbed."

Lieutenant Ives was a competent officer but certainly one of the world's worst prophets. Not much more than a hundred years later, his "profitless region" destined to be "forever unvisited" is nowadays visited by hundreds of thousands every year coming from as far away as Europe and Asia principally to see for themselves this uniquely beautiful and uniquely instructive wonder of nature.

To the majority of those who come, gasp, admire and then go away with a memory that will never fade, the Canyon is simply a stupendous spectacle. One stands at the rim and one gazes into the great gulf out of which rise the fantastically colored and fantastically carved buttes which inevitably suggest the temples of southeastern Asia. Only from a few points, here and there, can one glimpse the river far below, but whether one sees the river or not the changing lights and shadows make a spectacle differing every hour of the day from dawn to dusk.

The photographs in this volume describe far better than any words can, the majesty of the spectacle. They also reveal a great deal more than the casual visitor will ever see. The "Visitors Center" may be reached over first-class highways and the mildly adventurous can join a caravan which daily threads its way down the winding trails to the river running a mile below the rim. But few ever stray dangerously aside from well-trodden paths. Considered as a whole, the Canyon is one of the least visited as well as one of the most visited spots on earth. By now the often unscalable banks of the river are fairly well known, but there are many square miles which have probably never been trod by a white man's foot. Hence, the photographs in this volume depict beauties the tourist never sees and provide also stunning vistas of the Canyon's setting in a desert landscape thickly studded with the fantastic and fantastically beau-

tiful sandstone buttes, which have been weathered (mostly by wind-blown sand) into imposing monuments which suggest irresistibly the ruins of some ancient city.

What has made the difference between the attitudes of Cárdenas or Ives and that of today's visitors is, of course, in part the safety, convenience and comfort which the present-day traveler enjoys. A hundred years ago, the area was roadless, unmapped and over large areas waterless. The explorer cut off for months from civilization risked death by thirst or at the hands of hostile Indians. He felt himself at the end of the world to whose habitable regions he might never return. Today's vacationist arrives by perfect roads and lodges in comfort as well as safety.

But there is another, if related reason for the changed attitude. When most of America and much of Europe was empty and untamed, men fled from wild places. Mountains and deserts were then "horrid", not, as they presently began to become, "sublime". The scarcer untamed wilderness, empty space and unspoiled nature became, the more they were sought for. This changing attitude is already beginning to be evident when in 1869 Major Powell dared the unknown dangers of an unmapped, turbulent and boulder-strewn river to float his group of rafts down the whole length of the Canyon. It was he who first referred to "Grand Canyon", not simply as men had been accustomed to say "the Big Canyon". And the change is significant. It is also important that he was a scientist who began to describe the geological significance of what he had seen. But it was no less significant that what had been to Cárdenas merely a frustration was already becoming an exciting adventure and an esthetic experience, as well as a dangerous enterprise.

In 1903 President Theodore Roosevelt, one of the first Americans who realized that the time had come when our problem was no longer that of conquering the wilderness but of preserving some of it, visited the Canyon and declared:

11

"In Grand Canyon Arizona has a natural wonder which, so far as I know, is in kind absolutely unparalleled throughout the rest of the world... Leave it as it is. You cannot improve upon it. The ages have been at work on it, and man can only mar it. What you can do is to keep it for your children, your children's children, and for all those who come after you as one of the great sights which every American, if he can travel at all, should see."

Sixteen years later, the most spectacular portions of the river and much of the country surrounding it became one of the most spectacular of our national parks and as such is as well protected as can be from commercial exploitation and vandalism. Only recently, however, a proposal to establish two power dams, which would have drastically altered the appearance and ecology, was defeated only after a vigorous battle. We can only hope that some such battle will not someday be lost. Meanwhile, as Mr. Heiniger's photographs so effectively demonstrate, it is still a place where we can see one of the most beautiful spectacles that nature, unaided and undisturbed by man, has created for the delight of those of us who can appreciate it.

Joseph Wood Krutch†

12

**Relief Map of the
United States of America
Scale 1 : 13,000,000**

# Geography, Geology and History

*First encounter.* The first encounter with a landscape in many respects resembles that with another person. I first heard about the Grand Canyon in a lecture theater of Clark University in Massachusetts. An inspired and inspiring teacher, Professor Wallace W. Atwood Sr., gave us students a description of the personality of the Grand Canyon in its general outline and in its geological and morphological detail. Afterwards we had to work through maps and a reading list, and in the end we really believed we knew the Grand Canyon. Undoubtedly our knowledge would have been sufficient to pass an exam. And yet we were wrong: an encounter with the Grand Canyon is no different from an encounter with another person. No matter how much has been heard about him from others, something always remains unsaid or not understood, something which frequently, upon the first direct encounter, impresses us most deeply and indelibly.

For me this experience came at a time when the South Rim of the Grand Canyon was still comfortably reached by rail from Williams. A spur line of the Atchison, Topeka and Santa Fe Railroad made this a feasible detour from a journey between Los Angeles and Chicago. In the early hours of the morning we traveled north through increasingly thick pinewoods, gradually rising to over 6,500 feet. The country is mainly flat once one has passed the volcanic mountains near Williams; its base is composed of horizontal layers of Permian limestones. Vegetation and soil color indicate aridity. Behind us the San Francisco mountains reach heights of up to 12,659 feet and show evidence of recent volcanism. The landscape we are traveling through, on the other hand, forms part of the sedimentary Colorado Plateau and is locally known as the Coconino Plateau. Its few drainage troughs do not run northward towards the Grand Canyon but unite somewhere toward the south-west and only eventually, by a roundabout route, become tributaries of the

Colorado. The further we go the flatter the Coconino Plateau becomes and there is nothing in the least to suggest the proximity of the Grand Canyon. Finally the train stops in the middle of the tall forest: we have reached the end of the line. Nowadays this is a busy tourist center but when I first arrived there I was surrounded by peace and quiet and believed myself to be at the world's end.

A few steps take us from the railroad track to the slightly elevated timber structure of the El Tovar Hotel and to the edge of the Grand Canyon. These few moments mark one of the most striking changes of scenery imaginable. Abruptly, without any warning, one stands at the precipice of the Grand Canyon and one's gaze roams across it to the Kaibab Plateau, the North Rim. This first direct encounter reveals the personality of the Grand Canyon in a more impressive manner than even the most perfect academic or poetic account could achieve.

This is a unique experience. Naturally one can try to repeat it—but it can never be the same again. The most one can do is enable others to share the same experience. Thus, years later, I took my family to the Grand Canyon. Full of surmise but without any clear idea we encountered this grand spectacle of nature. The impression once more was so overwhelming that one merely gazed and marveled, forgetting all the people around one and behind one. On this visit we spent two nights at the hotel in order to be able to stay the whole day at the Grand Canyon. This extends in an east-westerly direction and the face of the landscape, therefore, changes during the course of the day with the position of the sun. The first impression is that of size, the next that of variety. The coloring of the rock and the clarity of the view change with the time of day; even the profile of the rocky gorges seems to participate in this magic transformation. The picture attains dramatic grandeur when the sky is
darkened by an approaching storm and when lightning flashes.

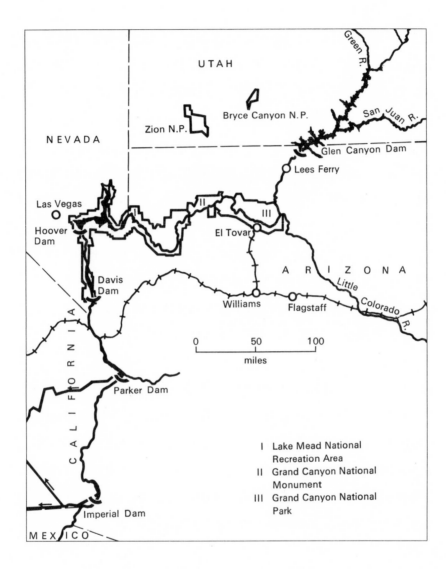

Fig. 1: General Survey. The sketch map shows those sectors and localities which are discussed in the text. The river's upper reaches and estuary lie outside this map section.

I   Lake Mead National
    Recreation Area
II  Grand Canyon National
    Monument
III Grand Canyon National
    Park

It is possible at the Grand Canyon to go in for what is nowadays called active tourism, to descend into the depths on muleback, to race across the plateau deserts in buses, to be instructed by rangers in all that is beautiful and interesting. It remains my firm conviction that, in order to gain any measure of familiarity with the Grand Canyon at all, one must gaze at it calmly for at least a whole day, from early morning until late at night. There are landscapes just as there are people whom one gets to know better and who communi-

19  cate better if one can listen to them in silence.

It is always interesting to compare one's own impressions and views with those received by others. Clarence Edward Dutton, the author of "The Tertiary History of the Grand Canyon District, with Atlas" (1882) writes:

"It is never the same, even from day to day, or even from hour to hour. In the early morning its mood and subjective influences are usually calmer and more full of repose than at other times, but as the sun rises higher the whole scene is so changed that we cannot recall our first impressions. Every passing cloud, every change in the position of the sun, recasts the whole. At sunset the pageant closes amid splendors that seem more than earthly."

Before me lies a small volume, published in 1926, entitled "Gran Cañon—My Visit to the American Wonderland". Its author is none other than the famous explorer of Central Asia, Sven Hedin. He visited the Grand Canyon at the invitation of the Santa Fe Railroad Company in 1923. He, too, came by rail from Williams. This is how he recorded his first impressions:

"A few minutes later the train stops at El Tovar and cars take us up to the hotel. It is only a few minutes drive, a few hairpin bends, and before one realises it the car drives up in front of the south-facing verandah of a fairly large brown wooden building, in rustic style, two storeys high and reminiscent of a tourist hotel... There is nothing here to suggest the Gran Cañon; the hotel building blocks one's view."

Being a guest of honor Sven Hedin was first conducted into the hotel and hospitably treated. Only then was he allowed to view the

Grand Canyon.

"After a meal with Birchfield and Kemp in the crowded dining room the three of us drove out to some of the nearest viewing points on that first evening... The sunset colors began their spectacle... One does not speak to one's companions, one shakes one's head and asks oneself if this is real or a dream. In vain does one try to comprehend the dimensions. It is very nice to be told that the distance to the North Rim is 13 kilometers and that the Colorado lies 1,500 meters below us. But this does not help. All dimensions and distances seem so enormous. When one steps to the edge of the Gran Cañon one believes that a huge chunk of the earth's crust is missing. It is as though the Creator, when fitting the solid land together on this earth, had forgotten to fit the last piece of the jigsaw, leaving a yawning empty space in its place."

The white man's first encounter with the Grand Canyon was entirely different, and so were his thoughts and feelings. We have a record of these in the "Relación de la jornada de Cibola conpuesta por Pedro de Castañeda de Nacera... la cual fue el año de 1540", available also in French (H. Ternaux-Compans) and English translations (14th Annual Report of the Bureau of Ethnology, 1893). In this account Castañeda described the important journey of exploration which the Viceroy of Nueva España commanded Francisco Vazquez de Coronado, a conquistador from Salamanca, to carry out in the south-west of what is today the United States between 1540 and 1542. Broadly speaking, this expedition covered the area from the Gulf of California through the southern part of the present states of Arizona and New Mexico eastward into the plains of Texas. The town of Cibola in the title was an Indian settlement on the lower reaches of the Colorado about whose wealth fantastic reports were circulating in Nueva España and which therefore was the first main destination of the expedition. Coronado's expedition passed south of the Grand Canyon. On August 25, 1540, however, the leader despatched a special party under the command of Don García Lopez de Cárdenas in a northerly direction to verify reports about the existence of a big river. In September this party reached the South Rim of the Grand Canyon—the exact spot is still the object of interpretation attempts by scholars—and far below them caught sight of the brown Colorado of whose dimensions, however, they were quite unable to form a correct idea. They had a good deal of trouble with the aridity of the Coconino Plateau and the lack of water; Cárdenas himself went out to search for water each day. A party of three was instructed to attempt the descent into the gorge down to the river. We even know the names of two of these men—Juan Galera from Almendralejo and Captain Pablos de Melgosa from Burgos. They, too, suffered from water shortage and returned before being able to reach the river. They reported on huge rocky boulders lying in the ravine; these, they said, were taller than the *torre mayor*—the famous Giralda—of the Cathedral of Seville. It appears that one of the members of Cárdenas's party, Pedro de Sotomayor, kept a diary but this has not been found to this day.

It seems that the Grand Canyon made so little impression on the Spaniards that they did not even give their new discovery a name of its own. True, they had previously named the lower reaches of the Colorado at the Gulf of California: it was known either as the Rio de Buena Guia—referring to the motto in Viceroy Mendoza's coat of arms—or the Rio Tison, referring to torch-bearing Indians. Cárdenas's party realized that the river in the depths of the canyon must belong to the Rio Tison system, but they were not sufficiently interested to give it a special name. Nowadays we know the various names which the Indians had given the Colorado. For them it played an important part and a number of Indian settlements exist

to this day on the basis of irrigated cultures in protected positions in the depths of the gorge. In two instances the river's Indian name refers to its red-brown color. To the Spaniards the canyon was principally a topographical barrier to any northward extension, a frontier whose efficacy was further strengthened by the inhospitable climate, the aridity and the cold winter.

Juan de Oñate, resuming the Spanish exploration of the south-west a good half century after Coronado (1604), used the name Rio Grande de Buena Esperanza for the lower reaches of the Colorado. A tributary of the Colorado, joining the principal river a short way above the canyon and draining vast regions of eastern Arizona—nowadays called the Little Colorado River—was labelled Rio Colorado by Oñate. "Colorado" did not mean colored or colorful but red or reddish-brown. It was not a bad label because after heavy downpours the river's water is noticeably tinted by the strongly colored rock and soil material which is readily washed away from the desert-type catchment area. Because of this marked coloration of the rock part of this catchment area it is nowadays called the Painted Desert. The Little Colorado is not the only tributary which possesses this characteristic but it has always possessed it to a particularly marked degree. Deep down in the Grand Canyon there is now a hydrological station where the suspended load—i.e. the quantity of solid matter carried in suspension—is measured. The daily average so far has been roughly 500,000 tons. On one occasion, however, during a flood in 1927, a value of 27.6 million tons was reached. From such measurements it is possible to calculate the scale of erosion—about 2 cm (¾ inch) on average per century—as well as the rate at which reservoirs built downstream are filled. It should be remembered that no measurements are available for the volume of material transported in solution or as gravel on the river bed. No doubt the load of gravel is also considerable and of particular

importance in assessing the river's erosion capacity. Nowadays the principal river is blocked above the Little Colorado confluence by the Glen Canyon Dam (Lake Powell) and has in consequence become "cleaner". The mean suspended load at the hydrological station has dropped to approximately 80,000 tons per day, and only when there has been heavy rain in eastern Arizona does the Little Colorado again carry large quantities of red-brown water.

Oñate's name Colorado was presently used increasingly also for the main river. Early American texts often also use the English translation Red River; to avoid confusion it was referred to as the Red River of the West or Red River of California. After the present Southwest had been ceded to the United States by Mexico the designation Colorado River for the main river became official, at least as far as the confluence of the Green River and the Grand River in eastern Utah. Not until 1921 did the US Congress decide that the Grand River was in the future to be called the Colorado River. This concern with nomenclature is interesting and instructive. It not only points to hydrological peculiarities but also reveals the significance which its discoverers attached to the river and the character with which they invested the landscape. Francisco Tomas Garces, a Franciscan and missionary, in 1776 called the Grand Canyon ravine a *calobozo,* a prison, or a *puerto,* a bottleneck for the river forcing its way through the rocks. In honor of the Viceroy of Nueva España he called it Puerto de Bucareli.

Lieutenant Joseph Christmas Ives (1857), on an official mission to explore the newly acquired territories, used the official name Colorado and Canyon. But he too was scared off by the wild character of the scenery:

"The region is, of course, altogether valueless. It can be approached only from the south, and after entering it there is nothing to do but leave. Ours has been the first, and will doubtless be the last party of whites to visit this profitless locality. It seems intended by nature that the Colorado river, along the greater portion of its lonely and majestic way, shall be forever unvisited and undisturbed."

As during the Spanish era, the Colorado remained a barrier several hundred miles long. The roads to the West passed far to the south of it or else had to make a northerly detour of hundreds of miles. Only sporadically did some Mormons, coming from the north, feel their way forward into this region and indeed settled there. The best known among them was John Doyle Lee who in 1871 accomplished the only crossing of the Colorado by ferry above the canyon reach. Lees Ferry has remained to this day an important point on the Colorado. It is conventionally regarded as the boundary between the upper and lower part of its catchment area.

The manner in which humans react to a landscape depends on the time of the encounter and on subjective factors. In the last section of this chapter we shall touch on the importance which the Grand Canyon of the Colorado has attained, as a National Park and a spectacular demonstration of natural evolution, for millions of people coming from an urban society, an importance which neither Cárdenas nor Lieutenant Ives could suspect and which in many respects is also far removed from the quiet dialogue already mentioned.

*Exploration.* In 1848 Mexico ceded the territory of the present Southwest to the United States of America. We have already mentioned the official naming and Lieutenant Ives's expedition which resulted from this transfer. But the large-scale connections of river and mountain systems remained to be clarified and only slow progress was made with the surveying and accurate topographical map-

25

ping; indeed these may be regarded to this day as not wholly concluded. We shall deal later with the general significance, in terms of the history of science, of the elucidation of conditions in the West. For the moment we shall confine ourselves to two particularly important achievements—the exploration of the canyon reach of the Colorado by John Wesley Powell and the first detailed geological study of the Grand Canyon territory by Clarence E. Dutton. Readers in the Old World should always remember that these expeditions and explorations were taking place at a time when the Franco-Prussian War was raging and European industrial economy was beginning its steep rise.

John Wesley Powell was born in the Middle West in 1834 and at an early age turned to the study of natural sciences, especially geology. In the Civil War he enlisted on the side of the North in 1861, lost his right arm in action in the following year and in 1865, at the end of the war, was discharged with the rank of Major. He has since become known as Major Powell. He owes his fame to his bold explorations on the Colorado River between 1869 and 1872. He embarked on his first voyage at Green River, Wyoming, on May 24, 1869 and accomplished it in one go. Its purpose was to prove that it was possible to navigate the Colorado by boat along its entire canyon stretch (see Figure 2). Major Powell has this to say in his account:

"May 24, 1869: The good people of Green River City, Wyoming, turn out to see us start. We raise our little flag, push the boats from shore and the swift current carries us down."

Green River was chosen as the starting point because it was a stop on the Union Pacific Railroad which had started operation a few
26 years before. The boats and all the material needed by the expedi-

tion could therefore easily be brought to the starting point. Prior to the railroad age Green River had been a welcome stopover for thousands of people who crossed Wyoming by the Oregon trail in order to reach the Northwest of the present United States or California.

An official army map printed in 1868 showed the correct arrangement—though with distorted proportions—of the course of the Green River and the Colorado Grande a short way beyond Lees Ferry. In the canyon sector itself, down to the big bend near Las Vegas, on the other hand, the river course was shown only by a dotted line and the higher parts of the Colorado Plateau to the west and north of the river, in the states of Arizona and Utah, were left entirely blank. A survey map of the western United States printed by Samuel Bowles at Hartford, Connecticut, in 1869 admittedly no longer contained any blank spaces and showed the river course by a continuous line, as well as the names Green River, Grand River, Colorado River and Great (not Grand) Canyon, but these innovations are probably due more to the difference between official and commercial map production than to an increase in topographical knowledge. Major Powell's voyage was a bold adventure, a foray into unknown territory along a wild and dangerous stretch of river. Anyone wanting to know more about this should read the report subsequently published by him. When the perils had been survived and the first camp struck at the end of the canyon stretch, Major Powell wrote as follows:

"Now the danger is over; now the toil has ceased; now the gloom has disappeared; now the firmament is bounded only by the horizon; and what a vast expanse of constellations can be seen! The river rolls by us in silent majesty; the quiet of the camp is sweet; our joy is almost ecstasy. We sit till long after midnight, talking of the

Grand Canyon, talking of home, but chiefly talking of the three men who left us. Are they wandering in those depths, unable to find a way out? are they searching over the desert lands above for water? are they nearing the settlements?"

Those three companions who had left the expedition of their own accord at one of the most dangerous moments, had by then fallen victim to Indian attacks and were never to return home.

In 1870 Major Powell explored the parts of the Colorado Plateau north of the Grand Canyon with a view to preparing a second expedition. On May 22, 1871 he started his second journey down river, again at Green River. This time, however, far longer was spent on the exploration proper of both sides of the river and on surveying. At the approach of winter the voyage was interrupted at Lees Ferry and winter quarters were set up at Kanab in southernmost Utah. Exploration was resumed in the spring of 1872, the Grand Canyon was again navigated, but on September 8, 1872, the voyage was cut short at the confluence of the Kanab River.

Major Powell first reported on his two expeditions in "Scribner's Monthly" (1874–1875) and presently in a comprehensive account "Exploration of the Colorado River and its Tributaries" (Smithsonian Institution, Washington, 1875). The main report was re-published in 1957 by the University of Chicago Press and the University of Cambridge Press, and the so-called diary section was re-issued in 1969 by Dutton, with magnificent pictorial material, under the title "Down the Colorado". The account is a strange combination of events of both expeditions in only seeming chronological order—a circumstance which has been the subject of repeated criticism aimed at Major Powell by scholars. This choice of account will be more readily understood if one remembers that Major Powell

conducted his exploration not by official order but on his own initiative. This meant that he had to raise the necessary means himself, and for this he received the backing of railroad companies, scientific institutions, the army, etc. His account was designed to gain publicity for his enterprise, to enlist widespread financial support and quite generally to arouse interest in the exploration of the West. Major Powell made ample use of his freedom as an independent explorer: he deliberately dramatized his account and used a colorful style. Success and support were not denied him and during the next few years his explorations were extended chiefly into the parts of the plateau west of the Colorado. His account was also translated into foreign languages and became a favorite reading matter among young people.

Major Powell's interests were extensive. He soon became involved in the study of Indian communities, their language and customs. He founded the official Bureau of American Ethnology and from 1881 to 1894 was Director of the recently founded United States Geological Survey. His extensive knowledge of the possibilities of colonization in the arid West moreover led him to adopt an exceedingly critical attitude towards Washington's official land policy. Admittedly his views carried little weight at the time; in retrospect it can be stated that his criticism and his proposals for a more rational land policy were well founded and that many incorrect decisions could have been avoided had they been followed.

The first detailed geological investigation in the sector of the Grand Canyon dates from about the same time. True, provisional observations had already been made on Lieutenant Ives's above-mentioned expedition by John Strong Newberry, a qualified doctor but a geologist by inclination. Newberry was the first to realize that the Grand Canyon could probably provide more information about the

earth's history than anywhere else in the entire American continent.

Unfortunately the Civil War delayed the publication of Newberry's reports which, in consequence, lost a good deal of their topicality. Their examination, however, shows that he not only succeeded in making a wealth of observations but that he also developed some quite far-reaching ideas on the basis of these observations. This is the more noteworthy as that expedition did not primarily serve geological exploration and Newberry had only a short time available for evaluating whatever chance observations he might have made along the party's itinerary.

It was Clarence Edward Dutton, a collaborator and friend of Major Powell, who was commissioned by the United States Geological Survey to carry out a detailed exploration. For that reason his report was published in the large-size series of Government publications and bears the title "Tertiary History of the Grand Canyon District, with Atlas" (Washington 1882). Dutton had accompanied Major Powell on his expeditions in 1875 and therefore knew the region and its problems. His own investigations, the basis of the report just referred to, were made during 1880 and 1881.

In spite of its length Dutton's account still makes interesting reading in more than one respect. This is true, though in an entirely different sense, both of the text and the atlas volume.

As far as his text is concerned, Dutton deliberately abandoned the traditional style of reporting customary in geological works and more especially in official accounts, where matters are discussed very clearly but often very tediously. In view of the fact that Dutton had taken a degree in literature, one might think that the dry style of reporting had simply been alien to him. A critical comparison with other scientific papers of his, however, leads one to a different conclusion: clearly the special form of the text was here dictated by the subject itself. The unique character of conditions at the Grand

Canyon virtually compelled him to seek new paths of presentation, both in construction and style, in order to produce the right effect on the reader. Indeed Dutton states this very clearly in his preface:

"I have in many places departed from the severe ascetic style which has become conventional in scientific monographs. Perhaps no apology is called for. Under ordinary circumstances the ascetic discipline is necessary. Give the imagination an inch and it is apt to take an ell, and the fundamental requirement of scientific method—accuracy of statement—is imperiled. But in the Grand Cañon district there is no such danger. The stimulants which are demoralizing elsewhere are necessary here to exalt the mind sufficiently to comprehend the sublimity of the subjects. Their sublimity has in fact been hitherto underrated. Great as is the fame of the Grand Cañon of the Colorado, the half remains to be told."

It must also be remembered that Dutton was a most exact observer and made his deductions with caution. His self-chosen style, therefore, did not trip him up nor—to use his own words—did it have a scientifically demoralizing effect. His account of conditions is marked by a positively classic clarity and for that reason alone the reading of his account is a pleasure for any geologist or scientist. One of the reasons no doubt—and we shall resort to this point in the next section—is the fact that the discoverers of the West were able to stick to their own observations in the field and did not have to wrestle with pre-formulated doctrines or magisterial theories.

In the composition of this account, too, Dutton chose his own road. He takes the reader chapter by chapter from one point in the terrain to another and at each he describes and interprets the situation. In between these points a general theme is informally introduced and

31 developed. His account thus represents a complete break with the

conventional description in geological monographs which used to present the material under review first from a stratigraphical and palaeontological and then from a structural point of view.

But it is not only his style and presentation which makes his account interesting reading. In over 250 pages dealing with a narrowly limited area of the earth's surface, Dutton also discusses a large number of questions of general significance, questions which are valuable in terms of history of science. It is a great pity that nowadays we have less and less time for reading and that Dutton's work, together with other monographs of that great age of scientific field work, now gathers dust on library shelves.

It might be easier for us to pick up the accompanying atlas volume and leaf through it. This is remarkable in that, in addition to the topographical and geological maps, it contains a large number of unique lithographed representations of the scenery, some of them in color. The atlas is of an unusually large format (nearly 20 × 20 inches) and many of the plates are double-spread; all this helps to present the uniqueness of the landscape in a convincing manner. Such reproductions were also a vital prerequisite of the structure of the text chosen by Dutton, since only good reproductions—so he argued—were able to arouse in the reader the correct mental picture. Dutton did not himself draw the plates but had two important artists available to him.

One of these was Thomas Moran who had previously made the engravings for Major Powell's account. Moran was a well-known artist and one of his large paintings, ''The Grand Chasm of the Colorado'', had found a place of honor in the Capitol in Washington. Anxious though he was to portray nature faithfully, to convey the mood of the landscape seemed more important to him. Most of the pictures in the atlas, however, are not by Thomas Moran but by

William Henry Holmes. Holmes was less well-known as an artist and possibly also less important, but as a geological illustrator he seems to us greatly superior to Moran. With a precision suggesting the modern landscape pictures or geological profiles drawn by an autographic device, and with a clarity which matches the peculiar transparence of the dry mountain air far better than Moran's manner, Holmes created scenic pictures which to this day are among the best ever printed (see Figure 4). Holmes must have had a quite extraordinary understanding of geological structures and the forms of weathering. To draw such views one must first of all be able to see things correctly. Moran was certainly a draughtsman and a painter, but he lacked a geologically trained eye.

*Scientific conclusions.* The fact that the exploration of the West was important not only for its immediately valuable discoveries but also to the history of science, because of its great number of generally valuable conclusions, is still insufficiently known in the Old World. After a quick glance at the conditions under which research was able to develop, we shall discuss more particularly the contributions made by the explorers mentioned earlier in this chapter.

The first half of the past century saw the United States extend its territory to the Pacific and secure it against its neighbors to the north and south. In 1803 it purchased from France the catchment area of the Mississippi-Missouri from its estuary to its sources. In 1847 the Oregon Settlement brought in the Northwest and in 1848 the peace with Mexico the Southwest and California. The Republic of Texas, having recently detached itself from Mexico, had joined the United States in 1845. After a few minor frontier corrections the territorial extension of the United States was concluded within a few decades in what remain its frontiers to this day. One of the first

concerns of the Federal Government was to obtain a clear picture of the situation in the newly acquired western territories in order to frame a sound policy for their economic development on secure foundations. Sufficient information was probably available about former Spanish and subsequent Mexican territory. There was an extensive work published by Alexander von Humboldt in 1811, "Essai politique sur le royaume de la Nouvelle Espagne", in five volumes and an atlas volume. But these were only first beginnings and, as we have seen, vast regions remained *terra incognita* well into the second half of the nineteenth century.

The exploration of the western territories pursued entirely specific objectives. Among these priority was given, to begin with, to the establishment of the most favorable routes linking the East and the West. The unraveling of the river systems, the marking of the principal trails and eventually the construction of the railroad lines characterized the various stages of this endeavor. The Grand Canyon and the Colorado Plateau remained largely untouched. Only the Santa Fe railroad approached the territory in the south and opened it up with the Williams—El Tovar branch line.

The next task consisted in surveying the country and examining its economic potential. One of the first acts of the young United States was the formulation of a definite settlement policy in its western areas—i.e., beyond the former colonial territories or, in other words, west of the Appalachians. Standards were laid down for surveying and handing over land to the first settlers and these rules, apart from certain necessary modifications, have remained valid to this day. Simultaneously all territorial claims beyond the Appalachians were amalgamated to form the basis of the so-called Public Domain. All subsequent new acquisitions—excepting Texas—were added to this Public Domain unless legally valid claims to ownership were proved. The Federal Government thus not only possessed vast tracts of land but was also faced with the task of efficiently utilizing it. This involved not only allocation to settlers—whereby the land was transferred from federal to private ownership—but also various rights of use (prospecting and mining for minerals, use of forests and grazing, etc.), restrictions on use (nature reserves, Indian Reservations, etc.) and subsidies by land grants (to railroads, states, and public bodies such as universities, etc.).

Exploration, therefore, meant a great deal more than surveying and mapping. As we have hinted in connection with Major Powell's work, the scientist, in addition to drawing his maps, had to concern himself with geology, morphology, plant communities and wild animals; he had, moreover, to assess the region's utilization potential by white settlers and he frequently had to face the problem of the Indian communities and their integration into the modern age. At a time when the modern trend towards specialization was already well advanced in the Old World, the scientist in the American West was still confronted with the whole spectrum of problems.

The special task of efficient use of the Public Domain meant that certain questions were of particular importance. It must be remembered that, with few exceptions, the West is an arid region. Forest cover is found only in the Northwest and in the northern mountain sectors. In the Southwest the distribution of forests has not only an upper limit, imposed by the drop in temperature, but also a lower limit, imposed by the drop in humidity. Vast areas are grassland and desert, and hence without irrigation, usable only for extensive grazing and often only during certain seasons.

These natural geographical conditions, however, proved most beneficial to geological and morphological research. In the wooded East and also in the Middle West scientists were only able to gain an insight into the structure of the earth's crust at a few natural or artificial exposures. In the West, with no vegetation cover or only a very thin one, it was often possible to trace rock structures over hundreds of miles with a clarity which left nothing to be desired. It is therefore not surprising if, in the exploration of the West, a large number of such data were amassed and presently interpreted to yield generally valid conclusions.

We have already remarked that conditions in the West at the time did not favor specialization. But we can go further than that. At a time when in the Old World the fellow scientists of these explorers were enjoying a particular image as highly respected professors and *Geheimräte,* the explorers of the West differed from them also in outward appearance—moreover, from the point of view of an intellectual and cultured society—in an unfavorable manner. Long-haired, with bristling beards, in often untidy clothes, mounted like cowboys or trappers, rifle at the ready—that is how they appear in photographs and in popular tradition. They had to be able to do things which were never demanded from the professors or *Geheimräte* across the ocean. They had to know how to shoot and kill—not only wild beasts but if necessary also humans. They had to be able to carve up their quarry and to prove themselves competent cooks. If they were not to die of thirst they had to have an unfailing sense of orientation to find the waterholes. In short, their activity was a great deal more varied than one might think at first.

But one must not be deceived by outward appearances. As a rule these scientists had received excellent training, and after years of field work they often, later in life, attained important positions in universities or Government service.

We have already mentioned that John Strong Newberry was a doctor of medicine who became a geologist through inclination. He lived from 1822 to 1892. After the end of the Civil War he did not resume his interrupted field work but, as professor of geology at the Columbia School of Mines, entirely devoted himself to stratigraphy

and palaeontology.

Ferdinand Vandeveer Hayden (1829–1887), whom we have not yet mentioned, had also been a doctor at first; from 1867 onwards, however, he worked for the Government as a geologist. His special field were the parts of the Rocky Mountains surrounding the Colorado Plateau; his observations made there and the general ideas derived from them proved of the utmost importance.

Robertson Marvine (1848–1875), a member of the great Hayden Survey, also had an academic education and taught at the Harvard Mining School.

We already know some aspects of the life of John Wesley Powell (1834–1902). It should be added here that, even before embarking on his expedition, his careful scientific training and his own research had earned him a professorship of geology at the Illinois Wesleyan University and at Illinois Normal University.

Clarence Edward Dutton (1841–1912) had studied literature at Yale University. For him, too, the Civil War had been a crucial experience: it had aroused his interest in geological research. As a collaborator of Major Powell he worked on the subject of the Grand Canyon for the United States Geological Survey, and later on questions of volcanism and seismology.

Grove Karl Gilbert like Dutton belonged to the closer circle of Major Powell. He lived from 1843 to 1918. He received his training as a scientist at the University of Rochester. When Powell took over the directorship of the Geological Survey Gilbert followed him to Washington as chief geologist. He owes his reputation chiefly to his later studies of the (nowadays vanished or greatly reduced) quaternary lakes in the Rocky Mountains (Lake Bonneville and others). These monographs became classics of geological and morphological literature.

Among the better known people Jacob Hamlin, a Mormon and
37 missionary, was the only one without a university education. He

was a man respected and trusted by the Indians. Because of his expert knowledge of the region he served Major Powell as a companion but did not take part in scientific research.

Among the principal publications the following deserve mention in the present context:

J.W. Powell: Exploration of the Colorado River of the West— 1869–1872 (1875)
Report on the Geology of the Eastern Portion of the Uinta Mountains (1876)

C.E. Dutton: The Physical Geology of the Grand Canyon District (1880–1881)
Tertiary History of the Grand Canyon District, with Atlas (1882)

G.K. Gilbert: The Colorado Plateau Province as a Field for Geological Study (1876)
Report on the Geology of the Henry Mountains (1877)

Most of the listed items appeared in the series of the United States Geological Survey, in folio and, according to the usage of the time, bound in leather. They can be found in all major libraries. The most significant point in retrospect is that all the above scientists were breaking new ground. As a rule they had to begin by tackling geodetic questions and the mapping. Next came the collection of data and the recording of their findings in the form of thematic maps. On the basis of this reliable first-hand knowledge it was possible to proceed to general conclusions. Here was an important difference from work in those fields where researchers already had available to them important foundations and well-defined theories and where discussion of what had already been published frequent-

ly took up more time than the performance of new observations.

The most important research was done on behalf of the Geological Survey. This meant that the work was funded for a number of years. The individual researchers, moreover, had the opportunity within the framework of the organization of comparing their results with those of other workers. Finally, publication and extensive dissemination of the results were ensured.

The researcher in the West differed in a number of ways from his academic colleagues in the East of the United States and in the Old World. His working method, primarily, was the inductive method which proceeded from individual findings to general conclusions, whereas his counterpart would give preference to deduction. His work was increasingly conducted within the framework of a Government organization and not in the freedom of a university campus. His situation compelled him to consider nature and man in their overall pattern; specialization only developed at a later period of scientific study. It would be interesting to pursue the question of the extent to which the very different living conditions affected scientific work and the formulation of generally valid theories and ideas: on the one hand the perilous life in the Wild West, often in the company of rough and uneducated helpers, and on the other the position of a respected professor within the setting of a university or academy, in an atmosphere of erudition and culture.

Anyone wishing to form an idea of the wealth of generally applicable results produced by the above-mentioned researchers was obliged, until quite recently, to refer to the original publications. Nowadays such an interest is more easily satisfied. In 1964 a carefully documented publication by Richard J. Chorley and others appeared, entitled "The History of the Study of Land Forms or the Development of Geomorphology". The first volume contains a tribute to American research in the West; this has closed a perceptible gap in the literature.

In the Old World the picture was dominated by academic discussions about existing theories which, from time to time, were enriched by newly supplied data. For this reason one invariably finds various so-called schools confronting each other. In a survey of the history of scientific thought it is therefore possible to arrange these ideas in terms of schools or theories. In the West this method fails for obvious reasons. The individual researchers, as we have shown, proceed along inductive paths and, just because they always base themselves on pure observations, arrive at ideas which differ but slightly from one another. It is not therefore surprising if we find it difficult to ascribe a definite idea to one scientist only. It is of course possible that one of them first clearly formulated or published it. But in fact one finds that, uttered or not, there is an astonishing agreement among ideas and a continuous line running through them. Chorley's book perhaps does not pay sufficient attention to this fact and his textual quotations sometimes ascribe a certain concept to one particular worker.

To illustrate our point, the modern idea of climatically-conditioned morphological events can first be found in Newberry's reports. Powell in a detailed comparison explains how the land forms observed in the dry West would have developed in the more humid East under otherwise identical conditions, and he shows that it is therefore always necessary in the interpretation of an observed form to pay close attention to the climatic conditions under which it has developed. Dutton, too, devotes a good deal of space to this reflection. Nowadays climatic morphology is highly thought of and a good many living researchers believe that they are dealing with a new—not to say their own—invention. It is a pity, as we have said before, that few people find the time nowadays to read what earlier researchers have written.

Another important concept discussed and coined by Powell on the strength of direct observation is that of the "base level of erosion", the general degradation level. Here his observation proceeded from plateau surfaces subjected to continuous and vigorous erosion which he compared and equated with the surfaces of unconformity in the series of strata of the canyon. It was not until later that another American morphologist, William Morris Davis, coined the concept of the "peneplain" for this final surface of erosion. Although the term "peneplain" does not yet occur in Powell's writings, the entire content of the concept was already clear to him. All the above-named scientists paid a great deal of attention to the effects of crustal movements on the development of surface forms and in particular the drainage system. In this field Powell coined a whole series of concepts which have remained important tools of morphological work to the present day. Having demonstrated that, in one particular instance, the pattern of the drainage system must be older than the traversed structures he wrote: "I propose to call such valleys... antecedent valleys."

Among other types of such a genetic order Powell distinguished between consequent and superimposed valleys or river courses.

Dutton more particularly investigated the relative share of vertical erosion by flowing water and of slope weathering. An entirely modern touch both in his and in Gilbert's work is their attempt to present generally valid statements in the form of quantitatively expressed equations.

In a fundamental article Gilbert later (1886) had this to say about the method of circumstantial evidence (which is of particular importance in morphological research) and of a working hypothesis:

"A phenomenon having been observed, or a group of phenomena
41 having been established by empiric classification, the investigator

invents an hypothesis in explanation. He then devises and applies a test of the validity of the hypothesis. If it does not stand the test he discards it and invents a new one. If it survives the test, he proceeds at once to devise a second test. And he thus continues until he finds an hypothesis that remains unscathed after all the tests his imagination can suggest.''

We have singled out this passage because it shows that in America, too, in line with the progress of scientific knowledge and experience, inductive work was being increasingly replaced by deduction. This transition—especially in Gilbert—marks an important step in scientific history towards generally valid concepts, classifications and theory.

The list of contributions significant in this context could be extended a great deal. But we are more concerned to show that this period in the history of science occupies a special place than to explore every little detail of this aspect. Admittedly, only slight notice was taken in the Old World of this research activity. Apart from the reasons stated above, this was due, without any doubt, to a certain condescension toward "underdeveloped" America. Nowadays the situation has been reversed and it seems scarcely credible that there was a time when a European professor, speaking from genuine conviction, should tell a young student about to continue his studies in the States: "You will have an interesting time there but don't get the idea that you will derive much scientific benefit from it." It is also alarming to note the very slight attention paid to Powell, Dutton, Gilbert and others in European scientific work. A glance at bibliographies will bear this out.

It is too late now to do more than pay tribute to this work in
retrospect. Over the past hundred years research has made such

progress in every respect that the studies mentioned here have become classics in the word's truest sense. We still employ a whole series of concepts which were coined or developed at that time. William Morris Davis, the American morphologist and Harvard professor, subsequently championed several of these ideas also outside the United States. In 1908/09 he was invited by Albrecht Penck as a visiting professor to Berlin University. His lectures there appeared in 1912, in German, under the title "Explanatory Description of Land Forms". In this way his ideas about the morphological cycle, about the various phases in landscape evolution and about the peneplain as their end product, as well as many other problems, gained wide currency and today, accompanied by Davis's most instructive drawings, have become part and parcel of textbooks all over the world. Davis's work was mainly deductive because this was the simplest didactical method. This attitude reflected a certain theoretical stance and frequently made him the target of attacks.

*Cross section through geological history.* From the point of view of possible investigation the history of our planet may be divided into three phases. The beginning can be described only by comparison with other heavenly bodies and by working hypotheses. Then follows a period, measured in thousands of millions of years, whose phases are recorded in the rock strata. As we approach the present we can obtain additional information from surface formations. The best insight into rock strata is provided in tall mountains or in deep gorges of the type of the Grand Canyon, which is why Newberry calls this region the grandest exposure on the American continent. Here long periods of the geological history can be surveyed at a glance from a number of points. In a plain such a survey would
43  have to be performed laboriously by way of geological mapping.

The dimensions of the exposure at the Grand Canyon, in topographical respects, are as follows: the depth of the canyon ranges from 4,600 to 5,600 feet; the South Rim reaches a height of only 6,991 feet above sea level while the North Rim rises to 8,200 feet. The lowest point, near the hydrological station and the cable bridge across the Colorado, has an altitude of 2,501 feet above sea level. The width of the canyon between the two rims varies from 4 to 18 miles. The length of the river course within the Grand Canyon section is about 220 miles. If the entire canyon were filled with plaster of Paris and the cast tipped out upside down one would get a relief of the dimensions of the Apennines, though of lesser depth.

To anyone interested in the history of the earth one of the most impressive locations ever is Yavapai Point, thus named after an Indian tribe living in Central Arizona. Yavapai Point is reached from El Tovar in about 20 to 30 minutes by a comfortable trail immediately along the South Rim. There, several times a day, countless tourists assemble to have an employee of the Park Administration explain the landscape to them in what is the most magnificent schoolroom I have ever seen. What is so unique about this room is that the objects, models and rock samples displayed there, as well as the instructor's words, are directly related to the subject matter. A panoramic window provides a view of the canyon, down to its deepest gorges and across to the distant North Rim. Fifteen telescopes are permanently aimed at certain points in the terrain to enable each listener after the lecture to relate what he has just heard to what he is now seeing. The lecturers are specially trained for this work and are described as "naturalists". It is believed that more than 100,000 visitors a year make use of the opportunity of reading in this open book of superimposed rock strata the story of the origin
of the earth in general and of the Grand Canyon in particular, as

Figure 28.—Running a rapid.

Figure 79.—Section of wall in the Grand Cañon.

Fig. 2: Major J. W. Powell shooting the cataracts of the Grand Canyon on his expedition in 1869 (Powell, 1875).

Fig. 3: The geological structure of the Grand Canyon. A = Archean, B = Algonkian, C = Palaeozoic. Between B and C lies the "great unconformity" (Powell, 1875).

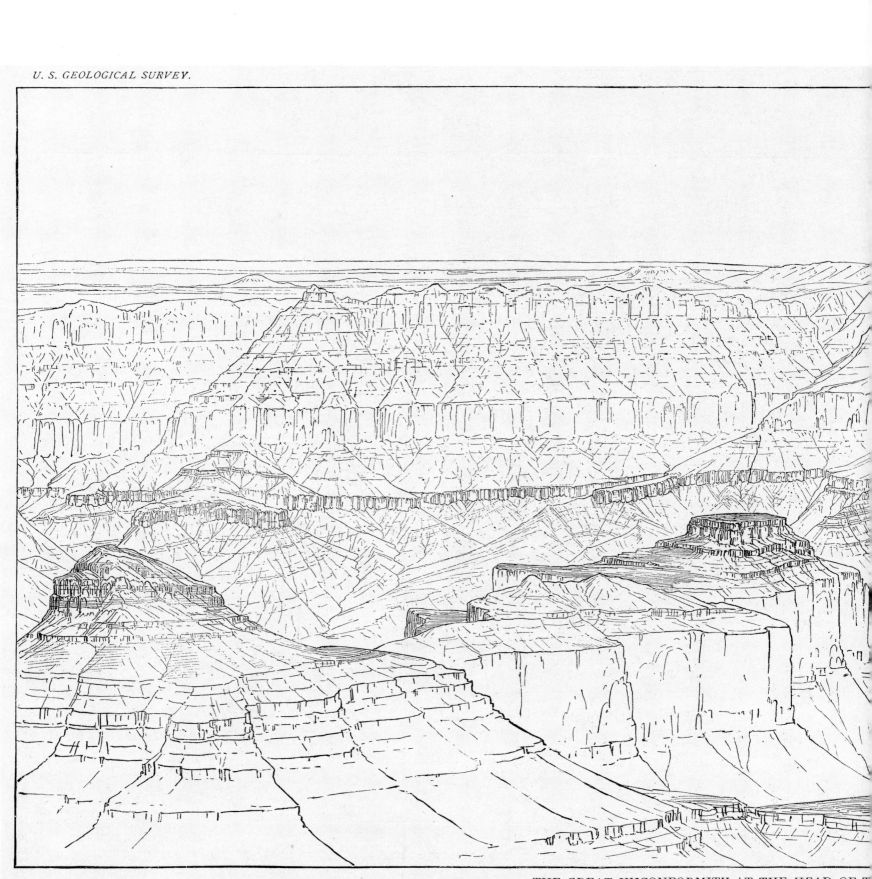

THE GREAT UNCONFORMITY AT THE HEAD OF T

Fig. 4: Geology of the Grand Canyon. W. H. Holmes drew the geological conditions in the upper part of the canyon, where erosion had not yet reached down to the Archean rocks of the Inner Gorge. Double-spread scenic sketch from Dutton, 1882.

*Dipping Algonkian*

Surface of unconformity

Tapeats sandstone

Redwall limestones

Coconino sandstone

Kaibab limestones

*Palaeozoic*

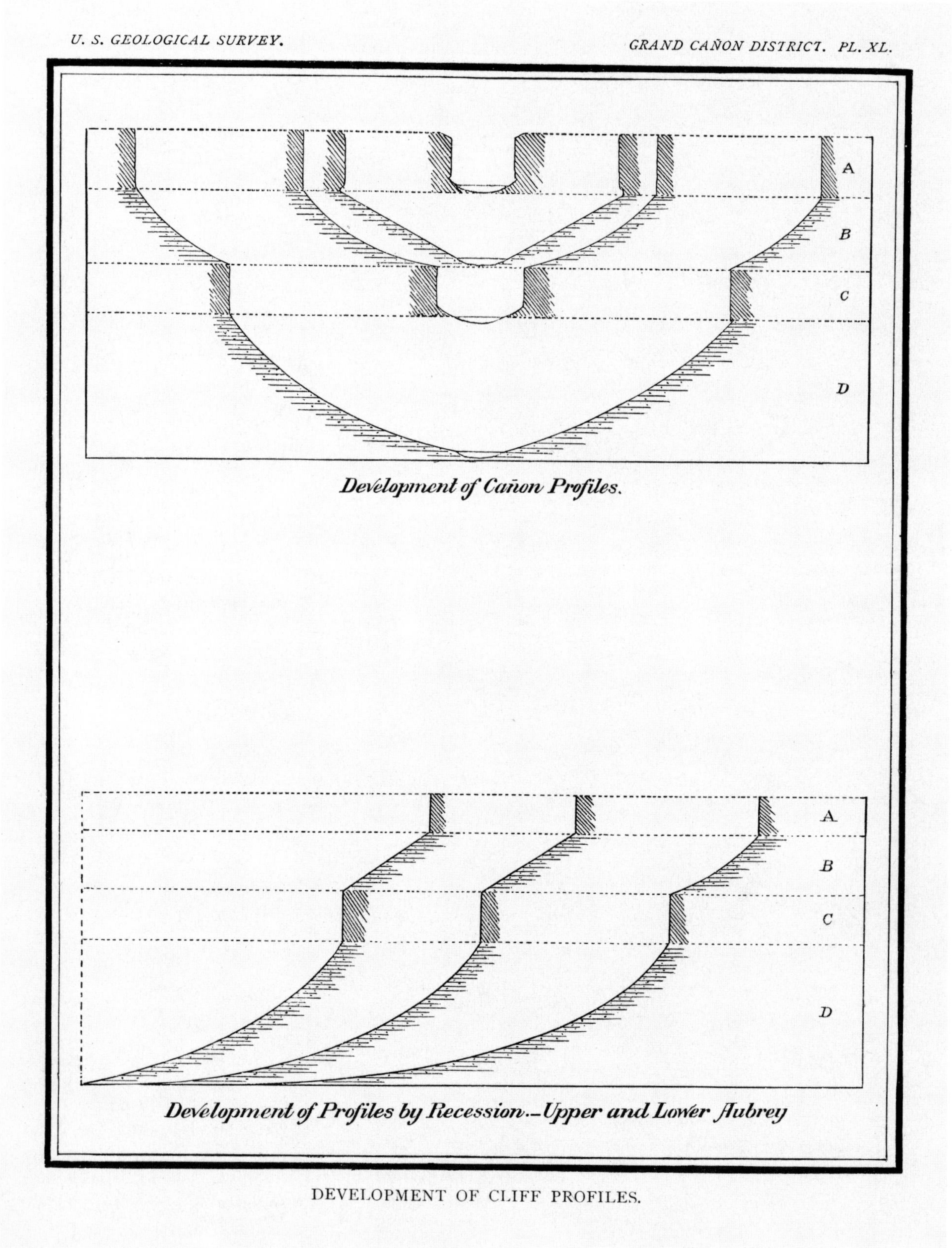

Fig. 5: Development of the theory of vertical erosion and the recession of profiles. The drawing comes from Dutton, 1882.

well as that of the evolution of life on earth. Let us now turn to the questions and to the answers provided by the canyon.

Rain wash—the removal of soil by water—can be observed on the plateau surfaces, and the transport of material in the river itself. This will eventually be deposited in the great plains and in the seas, whereby older deposits are continually covered by newer ones. This process, unless it is interrupted, results in a continuous profile of strata. The amount of denudation, the depth and temperature of the sea and other factors which can affect the character of the deposits can all change in the course of time. Whenever such changes exceed critical values the character of the sediments changes as well. Thus we find an alternation of limestone, sandstone and marl strata. The color of the rock can also change in connection with the color of the washed away material or due to chemical precipitation. Study of rock strata in an exposure enables us to draw a number of conclusions. We are able to distinguish older and younger rocks and to reconstruct the conditions prevailing at the time of sedimentation. These are the questions investigated by stratigraphy.

At Yavapai Point—as indeed at any other location on the South or North Rims of the canyon—we are on massive limestone, named Kaibab limestone after one of the great northern plateau regions. Kaibab is a word or concept from the language of the Paiute Indians and means something like "the mountain which has laid itself down", a truly picturesque description of a high plateau.

Looking down we notice that underneath the Kaibab limestones one rock stratum follows another in colorful alternation, some with vertical walls and others—less resistant—forming terraces. The entire profile (see Figures 3 and 4) has now been investigated and mapped. The most striking feature, to begin with, about 650 feet below us, is a more than 300 feet high vertical wall. This is formed by a layer of sandstone in which, somewhat as in dunes, a cross-stratification can be observed. Below these sandstones, for about 1,000 feet, are red marls and sand. The water running off them flows over a lower limestone horizon which forms a wall nearly 650 feet high, lending a reddish tint to the otherwise bluish-grey limestone. These so-called Redwall limestones and the higher Coconino sandstone are the most conspicuous strata in this series of rocks and are readily identified in all illustrations.

The whole series of sediments on top of which we stand at Yavapai Point appears to be running horizontally and undisturbed. Strictly speaking this is not so: our impression is an optical illusion. We said right at the beginning that the railroad to El Tovar gradually climbs from the south and runs all the way on top of the Kaibab limestones of the Coconino Plateau. The rock strata continue this upward inclination towards the north and the identical limestones on the North Rim lie roughly 1,300 feet higher than on the South Rim. The upper series of rocks, which we have so far discussed, is therefore gently tilted and rises towards the north, except that the amounts of uplift are so slight that they are not noticed from any one point at first sight. If, however, we look at the opposite side of the canyon then even a geologically untrained eye will instantly notice that underneath the so-called horizontal series there lies another one in which the strata are arranged obliquely like a wedge. While it is difficult at this distance to identify the character of the individual strata, the boundary between the upper horizontal and the lower dipping series is easily observed and traced over a great distance.

Lower still follows a rock in which we cannot detect any stratification at all. Seen from above it looks homogeneous and massive. It is into this rock that the so-called Inner Gorge of the Colorado with its virtually vertical walls has been cut.

Even without going into further stratigraphic details this three-fold 50 division (basic series, inclined sediments, horizontal sediments) enables important conclusions to be drawn as to geological history. These details are even more instructive if we take account of the traces of ancient life occluded in the rocks. These are problems of palaeontology which has supplied us with the history of the evolution of life as a yardstick for geological history. The combination of stratigraphy and palaeontology for a long time remained virtually the only means of arriving at valid statements about our planet's history. It is only quite recently that methods have been developed which enable us to convert the stratigraphic-palaeontological scale into years.

Thus the naturalist at Yavapai Point will first direct our attention to the bottom of the ravine and report that so far no traces of fossil life have been found in the rocks of the Inner Gorge. The age of these rocks has been determined as approximately 2,000 million years—an unimaginably long period. On closer examination, he will go on to explain, this seemingly homogeneous complex is found to consist of a great variety of rocks, folded and often standing upright, transformed into gneisses by pressure and heat. After his talk we shall be able to convince ourselves of the accuracy of his statements by examining the rock samples and stratigraphic profiles on show. He will next draw our attention to a limestone horizon (Bass limestone) in the superimposed inclined series. It is there—one telescope is focused on the precise point—that the oldest preserved traces of life have been found. These are calcareous algae of a kind existing to this day. The algae themselves, of course, have long been totally destroyed but the calcium carbonate secreted by them, revealing their characteristic structure, has survived.

According to the geologists' definition the basic series belongs to the Archean and the Bass limestones to the Algonkian systems. They are still considerably older than the Palaeozoic. The distinct

boundary between the Algonkian and the younger upper rock strata was clearly recognized even by the first researchers and described by Major Powell as the "great unconformity". This unconformity shows two separate events: first the Algonkian strata together with their base were forced into an inclined position, broken and also folded, and subsequently the terrain forms thus created were eroded into a vast plain. The "great unconformity" can be traced over a considerable distance and the extent of this degradation surface thereby demonstrated. Only later was the many hundreds of feet thick upper rock series deposited on top of this surface, and this upper series—apart from the above-mentioned tilting and a few fractures—was not subsequently disturbed. This early period of orogenesis and mountain degradation, which followed the Algonkian system, is described by American geologists as the "Grand Canyon Revolution" and has taken place 600 million years ago.

The strata of the upper and horizontal series right up to Yavapai Point belonged to the Palaeozoic. Here, too, occasionally a discontinuity of the stratigraphic series and erosion surfaces are found but these can be established only by detailed examination. Deposition evidently took place in a flat sea with the land at times rising a little above the surface. However, there was no more mountain formation. In the Palaeozoic strata fossils become increasingly frequent, showing the pattern of evolution encountered also elsewhere. Mussels and fishes have been found, and on land all kinds of plants and the tracks of amphibians. The terms used in America for the various strata differ somewhat from those customary in Europe but the general picture is the same.

At Yavapai Point we are on top of the most recent deposits of the Palaeozoic. If we consider that in other parts of the world—in the eastern United States and in Central Europe—mountains of the scale of the Alps were upfolded during the Palaeozoic we realise the uniqueness of the situation we can observe at the Grand Canyon.

The deposits of the Mesozoic and the Cainozoic eras, on the other hand, are totally lacking in the Grand Canyon profile. This means, to say the least, that no documentation survives of a span of time of roughly 230 million years. These strata, too, must have been deposited here at some time, at an estimated thickness of 5,000 to 10,000 feet. Following the uplifting of the Colorado Plateau the forces of degradation went into action and in the course of time removed all the more recent strata down to the level of the Kaibab limestones.

Mesozoic and younger strata are not found until we advance northward towards the high plateaus of Utah or eastwards to the structural basin situated in Eastern Arizona. To the east—in the area of the Little Colorado—we find in this basin, spared by degradation, widespread deposits of Triassic, Jurassic and Cretaceous formations. These are finely structured stratified rocks with a vigorous coloring of yellow, white, red and brown which have given the area the telling name of "The Painted Desert".

Moving north we remain for the best part of 60 miles on the plateaus formed by Kaibab limestones. Towards the Arizona and Utah state lines and beyond follow younger sedimentary series, in each case marked by an east—westerly cuesta. First of all we come to the Chocolate Cliffs of the Triassic formation, a series of strongly weathered unconnected high ranges. Roughly at the state line follow the Vermilion Cliffs, more than 90 miles in length and between 1,400 and 2,000 feet high. To the north and running parallel is the 1,000 feet high cuesta of the Jurassic White Cliffs. Here is the famous Zion Canyon and Zion National Park. Somewhat less high but particularly famous for their interplay of color and wealth of shapes along the deeply eroded cuesta follow next the Pink Cliffs and Cedar Breaks of Cretaceous and early Tertiary formations. The names borne by these striking scenic features indicate the unique character of the landscape. They do not possess the majestic grandeur of the Grand Canyon but make up for this by a greater wealth of bizarre forms and all kinds of natural spectacles. U.S. highway No. 89 makes it possible to combine a visit to the Grand Canyon with a visit to this fairy-tale world. While the South Rim of the Grand Canyon remains open to tourists throughout the year, the higher and more northerly Parks close their accommodation facilities during the winter months.

Many visitors enthuse more about Zion and Bryce Canyons than about the Grand Canyon. That is understandable. It depends on what one looks for. Bizarre and colorful landscapes in surveyable dimensions are found in greater number in the northerly Parks. But most visitors will take home with them a kaleidoscope picture, since without a geological map and considerable geological imagination it is downright impossible to grasp the connections.

The unique feature about a visit to the Grand Canyon—and especially to its South Rim—is that one single glance can take in, with convincing clarity, a coherent picture of an evolution which, measured in years, corresponds to the major part of geological history. It testifies to earlier mountain formations and the degradation of these mountains down to a peneplain. It takes us from the first beginnings of life on earth to the point when the animals conquered the dry globe.

Each visitor will have his own ideas of what is most impressive—and, as we have said, it depends on what he seeks.


*The Colorado River and the Colorado Plateau.* To get an idea of the size of the catchment area of the Colorado figures are not nearly so useful as a comparison with a familiar part of the earth. Whenever one superimposes two sections of a world map it is important to make sure not only that scale and projection are the same but also that a region of similar latitude and, if possible, likewise on the western side of a continent is chosen so that climatic conditions and regional characteristics determined by them are comparable. The most suitable region for comparison with the Colorado area is the western coast of Europe and Africa (see Figure 7, p. 61).

This would place the upper reaches of the Green River into the Cantabrian Mountains and those of the Colorado into Catalonia. Their confluence would be deep in the south of Spain, with Lees Ferry roughly near Huelva. The deserts in the estuary area at the Gulf of California would correspond to the southernmost coastal strip of Morocco. Just as Europe's Mediterranean rivers, the Colorado fluctuates greatly as to the amount of water it carries; this amount is decisive for the river's great erosive power. These fluctuations, however, are not only seasonal but may be observed over greater periods of time and this can be of vital importance for judging the irrigation potential and the allocation of amounts of water. The upper reaches lie in forest-covered high mountains which in winter are deep in snow. The major part of the region, just as in the European analogue, is arid territory, steppe and desert. Utilization of water for the needs of agriculture, industry and the cities is, in both hemispheres, at the centre of all development projects. But in the case of the Colorado the interest in water utilization extends beyond the catchment area: in the upper reaches water is "exported" eastwards into the foreland of the Rocky Mountains and from the lower reaches westwards into Southern California. We shall return to these problems of water utilization in the final section of this chapter.

Like most river areas, that of the Colorado is not of uniform origin but is composed of genetically different parts. The interpretation of the present pattern must be conducted with the aid of few pieces of evidence and largely on the strength of working hypotheses. That is

55

why J.H. Maxson, the author of the new geological map of the Grand Canyon (1968) writes with extreme caution:

"The time and method of development of the Colorado River and its course, from Rocky Mountains headwaters to the sea in the Gulf of California, have not been definitely established. Uncertainties and even inconsistencies make piecemeal explanation of sections of river course questionable. The stream pattern, canyon depth, and relative elevations of individual plateau segments seem to have been essentially established prior to the Pleistocene (1 million years ago)."

In the circumstances the skill with which the few pieces of available evidence are interpreted or the conviction with which a working hypothesis is presented can make all the difference. Equally important is the scientific authority of those supporting a particular view. This situation indeed could well be an obstacle to the discovery of the truth: in many respects it resembles the plea of a clever attorney who is concerned more with winning his case than determining the truth. Having examined the various views we therefore decided in favor of the following presentation:

About 40 million years ago, long before the beginning of the Pleistocene but after the deposition of the Mesozoic and early Tertiary sediment series discussed in the preceding section, the area of the Colorado Plateau in which the canyon sector is located (the Coconino-Kaibab Plateau) was upvaulted as a flat dome by forces in the interior of the earth and in this process fractured along certain lines. The result was a degradation of the younger and softer series above the Kaibab limestones in the zone of the upvaulting, a drainage pattern in line with the structural tilting and, along the fracture systems, considerable volcanism of the basalt effusion type.

To the west of the Kaibab dome or the Kaibab plateau—according to whether we refer to structure or topography we can use either term—the land was at first drained westward; all the water was then collected in a north-south channel and eventually reached the Gulf of California. The name Hualapai has been proposed for this drainage system. It coincides largely with the present-day course of the Colorado River from the Las Vegas bend to the estuary.

To the east of the dome we are interested above all in the sector below the confluence of the Green River and the Colorado. Here the proto-Colorado first flowed along the eastern flank of the dome, toward the south, in a similar position to the present river. Below Lees Ferry, however, it did not, as it does today, abruptly turn westward but continued its course with only a slightly veering toward the south-east. The present course of the Little Colorado River—but with a reversed direction of flow—probably corresponds to that of the proto-Colorado. It follows inescapably from this assumption that the Colorado at that time drained not into the Pacific but into the Gulf of Mexico. True, no evidence for this has been discovered. At the same time petrographic examination of sediments in the lower reaches of the present-day Colorado River—below the canyon sector and thus west of the Kaibab dome—indicates that no material from the region of the present-day upper reaches was carried there by Colorado water at an earlier period. Deposits were found whose age has been estimated at 20 to 30 million years in one case and 10 million years in another, and these testify to a still complete separation of an eastern and a western drainage system.

These calculations take us into the middle and late Tertiary period. At some point of time which cannot be established and along a line which can only be hypothetically assumed to have been west of the

57 Rio Grande the flow of the proto-Colorado in the direction of the

Gulf of Mexico was blocked by movements in the earth's crust and volcanic effusions. A vast lake was formed which no longer exists but whose existence can be proved by lacustrine deposits found over an extensive area in eastern Arizona, in the region of the Navajo Indian Reservation. The vanished lake has meanwhile also received a name—Lake Bidahochi. It is still surrounded by many mysteries. Was it a lake without outlet, undrained like so many lakes in Central Asia? Or did it have an outlet, and if so did it drain towards the Atlantic or the Pacific?

It is conceivable that at roughly this point of evolution the headward—i.e. retrogressive—erosion of the Hualapai system and the Lake Bidahochi waters urgently seeking an outlet encountered each other in the southern part of the Kaibab dome and thus determined the present course of the Colorado in the canyon sector. The separate parts of the system were fitted together and the Little Colorado reversed its direction of flow.

The great differences of altitude between the part east of the Kaibab dome and the western sector caused the river to carve its bed rapidly and vigorously from the confluence of the Little Colorado down to the Las Vegas bend and to produce a whole series of canyons. Subsequently the adjoining region upstream was likewise cut into by headward erosion. Nowadays there, too, one canyon follows another—first comes Marble Canyon, then Glen Canyon, Cataract Canyon (at the confluence of the Green River and the Colorado), Labyrinth Canyon, etc.

These, then, in rough outline, are the events which gave rise to the present Colorado River system, presented in a way which takes account of such evidence as is known to me. In this respect and with regard to the subsequent development I should like to seize on

three problems.

Investigations in the Grand Canyon have produced important results on the relative share of stream erosion and slope weathering, together with the problem of detritus removal. These questions were first discussed by C.E. Dutton in his monograph on the Grand Canyon (see Figure 5), in which he stressed the particular conditions of an arid climate. Seen overall, the proportion of the volume removed in the course of time by direct incision by the Colorado is probably slight. Nowadays stream erosion is effective only within the range of the Inner Gorge, i.e. the Archean rock series. All morphological occurrences above the terrace which forms the upper boundary of the Archean complex remain independent of stream erosion. Morphological evolution is instead governed by slope weathering, landslides and rain wash. Dutton formulated two important theses: the first states that gradient ratios, once established (rock face, terrace), are preserved in the course of evolution; his other thesis states that the rate of retrogressive weathering is independent of the size of the wall surface. Thus the scarp formed by the Redwall limestones, being a vertical wall, will weather retrogressively parallel to itself.

The second problem concerns the connection between structure and surface form. The North and South Rims of the Grand Canyon differ not only in their altitude—a difference readily explained by the upvaulting of the Palaeozoic series—but they also differ considerably in the degree of dissection of the canyon rims. Compared with the North Rim, the South Rim is less articulated or segmented. This is why the South Rim provides a deeper insight into the geological structures while the North Rim, for its part, offers the better general view. From Yavapai Point we can see, on the one hand, the suspension bridge deep down in the canyon providing the link with the far bank and the Phantom Ranch tourist center, while on the other we have a view up a side valley running into the canyon from the

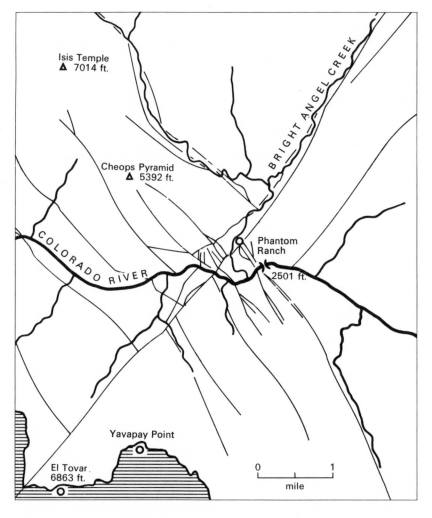

Fig. 6: Connection between fracture systems (thin lines) and river network. Comparison of the two line patterns clearly shows the high degree to which the course of rivers and hence of valleys—with the exception of the Grand Canyon—is predetermined by fracture structures.

*Map labels:* Isis Temple ▲ 7014 ft. · Cheops Pyramid ▲ 5392 ft. · BRIGHT ANGEL CREEK · COLORADO RIVER · Phantom Ranch · 2501 ft. · Yavapay Point · El Tovar 6863 ft. · 0 1 mile

north; this is Bright Angel Canyon and there is nothing to correspond with it on the south side. Bright Angel Canyon reaches deep into the northern plateau surface, dividing the Kaibab Plateau proper from the easterly Walhalla Plateau.

The geological map reveals that the rectilinear course of Bright Angel Canyon coincides with a series of fractures running in the same direction. Valley course and orientation of the fractures are clearly connected. The connection lies in the fact that along the fracture zones the rock was crushed and hence more readily attacked by weathering. The fractures are thus indirectly responsible

for the valley clearance.

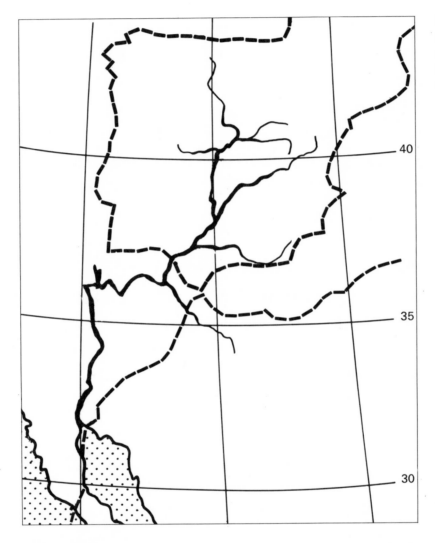

Fig. 7: The size of the catchment area of the Colorado River compared with that of the Iberian Peninsula and North Africa (the numbers are degrees of latitude).

The Bright Angel fracture system runs in a north-north-easterly direction. It is not the only one intersecting the Kaibab Plateau. Parallel bundles of fractures along the entire canyon stretch give rise to a series of canyons all of which run into the Colorado Valley from the north and some of which reach a great distance northward. The Kaibab Plateau in the wider sense is thus subdivided into individual sectors which all have their own names. Reading from west to east they are the Shiwitz Plateau, the Uinkaret Plateau, the Kanab Plateau, the Kaibab Plateau proper, and the Walhalla Plateau. The Kanab valley reaches farthest to the north. In it lies 61 the place where Major Powell spent the winter of 1871/72.

In addition to the north-north-east oriented fracture system there is another which extends towards the north-west. It marks the direction along which weathering has cleared the valleys of the second order. Both systems are particularly marked on the north side of the canyon. That is why their effect on weathering and terrain forms can be particularly well observed from the South Rim. Opposite Yavapai Point the massive block of the "Cheops Pyramid" and the "Isis Temple" are the result of erosional forces following the two fracture systems.

Not until farther north, immediately south of the Arizona-Utah state line, is the pattern of fracture-dictated topography overlaid and replaced by the east-west running cuestas mentioned above.

The third problem finally concerns recent volcanism. We have already mentioned the recent volcanic mountains near Williams and Flagstaff in the southern part of the Coconino Plateau. There some isolated effusions of basaltic lava occurred as recently as the 11th century, i.e. a relatively short time before the arrival of the first white man. Further to the north volcanism is absent from the area of the Coconino Plateau, but reappears north of the Grand Canyon in connection with the more frequent occurrence of fractures. It seems that, due to very recent earth movements some cicatrized wounds on the face of the earth were torn open again and once more began to bleed. In the Grand Canyon National Monument, which adjoins the Grand Canyon National Park at its downstream end, at Mount Trumbull, a lava flow first flowed into a northerly side canyon, Toroweap Canyon, and then as a powerful lava fall into the incision of the main river. The effusion is recent, more recent than any valley incision. In the Toroweap Canyon the lava flow blocked not only the occasional running water but also all the solid matter carried with it to a depth estimated at many hundreds of feet. In the canyon
62 the Colorado was temporarily ponded by a natural lava dam to form

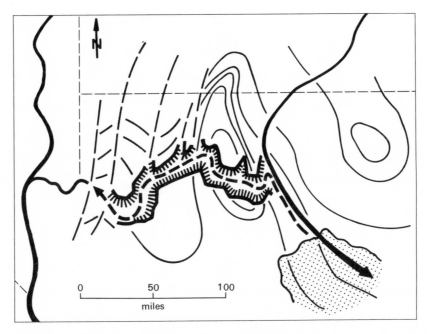

Fig. 8: Sketch showing the origin of the Grand Canyon sector (for explanation see the text).

a lake. The Colorado rapidly cut its way through this barrier and only a few remains still testify to this occurrence.

The past million years, roughly speaking, were a period of rapidly changing climatic conditions all over the earth. In Europe one speaks of glaciations and interglacial periods which repeatedly alternated. These climatic changes must be taken into account in the interpretation of the terrain forms observed if these are thought to have been formed during the period concerned. We have already pointed out that Major Powell and his co-workers attached great importance to these climatic-morphological considerations. Admittedly they were thinking chiefly of the peculiar features of arid climates compared with the more humid climates of eastern America rather than the palaeoclimatic conditions. It is interesting that so far only the traces of the last (Wisconsin) glaciation have been reliably established, and even these only on the high plateaus of the north. Could this mean that the Colorado Plateau was not raised to its present altitude above sea level until the Pleistocene and that the conditions for a glaciation of the highest parts were only created

63 during the last 100,000 years?

*Water Utilization—National Park.* According to official data the catchment area of the Colorado River covers 245,000 square miles and its length is 1,449 miles. Within the Grand Canyon National Park alone the length of the river course, because of its many windings, measures 105 miles; to this must be added another 40 miles within the Grand Canyon National Monument which adjoins it downstream. These few figures, together with what has been said so far, will convey an idea of the scale.

And yet the canyon sector is only a small part of the entire river system. Water utilization, however, concerns also this part, either directly or indirectly. So far it has fortunately been possible to prevent direct technological interference within the Park territory, even though—as we mentioned earlier—the construction of dams on the upper reaches has already had a measurable effect on flow and carrying capacity of the river. Conditions in the Grand Canyon cannot therefore be viewed in isolation from their wider context.

The catchment area of the Colorado is arid. Amounts of precipitation in excess of 20 inches are found only in the high mountain region of the upper reaches, and there a large part of the precipitation occurs in solid form during the winter and is not released until the spring thaw. About half the river area is desert or sparse grassland with precipitations of less than 12 inches. Greater amounts fall only on the higher parts of the plateau, for instance the Coconino and Kaibab Plateaus. There we find extensive areas of continuous forests.

We have already mentioned the peculiarities of Public Domain, land assignment and the grant of certain rights of usufruct. If we consider, quite apart from the general aridity, that the Colorado River and many of its tributaries flow through deep gorges it is not surprising that interest in permanent settlement has remained slight. About 70 per cent of the land continues to be in Public Domain, not having found any applicants for its use. Permanent settlement is possible only where there is an assured water supply—and that, without the construction of major technical installations, is the case at only a few points. On the other hand, the Government has granted mineral prospecting rights, grazing rights, etc., on a large scale. It has moreover designated considerable areas as Indian Reservations, as National Forests, as Parks and National Monuments, and more recently also for military purposes. It has also promoted an economically sound utilization of available amounts of water by financing dams and working out water distribution projects designed to guarantee an economic advance in the near future. These measures concern not only agriculture but increasingly also industry and urban settlements, as well as the important part played by running water in the removal of effluent. Conversion of water power into electric power represents another form of utilization. As a waterway, on the other hand, the Colorado no longer plays any part—unless one includes boat traffic in the recreation areas of the artificial reservoirs. Water has always been an asset in short supply and one that was bitterly fought over.

Seven states share in the river system of the Colorado. In terms of area percentage these are: Arizona 42, California 2.5, Colorado 16, New Mexico 9.5, Nevada 5, Utah 16 and Wyoming 8. The small remainder of 1 per cent goes to the estuary area in Mexico. After World War II the above-listed states concluded an agreement designed to regulate sensibly and fairly the utilization of available amounts of water. The agreement is known as the Colorado River Compact. It divides the river's catchment area into an upper and a lower half; the boundary is at Lees Ferry.

In the upper reaches there have not since been any major differences between the participants. The state of Colorado nowadays 65 diverts considerable quantities of Colorado water to the eastern flank of the Rocky Mountains, where it is urgently needed for urban consumption and for irrigation in the higher parts of the Great Plains. There is no need to touch on these conditions any further in the context of the present book.

Matters are different in the lower reaches, especially below the river bend at Las Vegas. Here the entire stretch within the United States, roughly 3000 miles, has been brought under control and into use by one hydroengineering installation after another. Immediately below the bend the Hoover Dam was built and a little further downstream the Davis Dam. They primarily serve the regulation of the water flow and the generation of electricity. The Hoover Dam backs up a vast lake, Lake Mead, which stretches back as far as the canyon sector without, however, reaching Grand Canyon; a northerly arm of the lake extends into the valley of the Virgin River. Further downstream is the Parker Dam. From there the Colorado River Aqueduct carries water to the Los Angeles and San Diego area. Just before the state boundary comes the last dam, the Imperial Dam, which, through the All American Canal, conducts water to the agriculturally important Imperial Valley. Clearly this sector of the Colorado River is utilized primarily by California; its water serves all sectors of the economy—cities and countryside, generation of power and, last but not least, recreation.

However, a major controversy has developed here between Arizona and California about their shares in river utilization. Arizona lags a good way behind California in economic development but its water and power requirements are growing from year to year. There is therefore a danger that the economic utilization of the Colorado will continue upstream and reach the area of the canyon. There is the possibility of a barrage at the upper end of Lake Mead. Compared

with the great length of the above-mentioned acqueducts into southern California the distances to the economically important area around Phoenix and the Gila River basin are within technically manageable dimensions. I have before me a plan which shows the project of a dam at this point. Its name is Bridge Dam. True, the lake backed up by it would not reach the central area of the Grand Canyon. On the other hand, the plan envisages the possibility of tapping Colorado water at a point below Lees Ferry and conducting it through a tunnel underneath the Kaibab Plateau to the upper end of this reservoir. It could be argued that, apart from reducing the amount of water deep down in the Inner Gorge, the territory of the Park would not be affected by this scheme; nevertheless this kind of development, if continued, is bound to clash with the interests of the Park.

In view of the quantity of solid material transported by the Colorado even Lake Mead would be filled in within about 200 years; already its efficacy is reduced by a definite calculable percentage each year. Two hundred years is a long period of time—but not really for investments on such a scale. Construction of dam installations further upstream (Glen Canyon Dam below the confluence of the San Juan River) have already succeeded in reducing the silting rate and extending by a multiple the useful life of the installations mentioned. An important requirement will be control of soil erosion and all its effects in the catchment area of the Little Colorado. We have already observed that this river now is primarily responsible for the quantities of mud and detritus. In 1950 a Special Commission's Report to the American President was published in which all these problems were presented in great detail ("Ten Rivers in America's Future"). As elsewhere on earth, the cause of conservation will have to fight hard to prevail. It represents values which cannot be assessed by the usual yardsticks and it is often shortsightedly accused of standing in the way of progress.

America's first National Park, Yellowstone Park, was created in Wyoming in 1872. A comparison between American and European National Parks reveals not only a different scale of magnitude and a different degree of inviolateness of nature but also certain more fundamental differences. In Europe a National Park is a total reserve from which humans are excluded as a matter of principle. In the United States, on the other hand, the law on the establishment of National Parks of August 25, 1916, expressly states that these territories are to be set up "to conserve the scenery and the natural and historic objects and the wild life therein and to provide for the enjoyment of the same in such manner and by such means as will leave them unimpaired for the enjoyment of future generations".

The word "enjoyment" occurs twice within this short quotation. An American Park is not a large-scale scientific experiment designed to restore or preserve a purely natural landscape but a region which it is hoped people will visit in order to renew their love of and acquaintance with nature and where, for this reason, such facilities must be provided as will enable them so to do. Such parks are set up wherever nature has something special to offer. So that this aim is achieved and preserved for future generations the Park territory is protected against all other kinds of interference.

In the case of the Grand Canyon it took decades before the idea, first mooted in the 80s of the last century, of creating a National Park on the lines of Yellowstone Park gained acceptance. In 1903 the then President, Theodore Roosevelt, visited the Grand Canyon and described it as "to me the most impressive piece of scenery I have ever looked at".

But even he was unable to get Congress to authorize the creation of 68 a Park. However, President Harrison in 1893 had designated an extensive area as the Grand Canyon Forest Reserve and thus, at least, prevented any seizure of land by settlers. In 1908 the establishment of the Grand Canyon National Monument ensured a ban on prospecting and mining for minerals. On February 26, 1919, at last, President Woodrow Wilson signed the Bill, passed by Congress, under which the Grand Canyon National Park was created. This meant that the administration of this territory was placed under the National Park Service of the Department of the Interior. The idea was to extend the Park territory as little as possible to the plateaus on both sides of the canyon. This territory was then roughly 56 miles long and 22 miles wide. Following an enlargement in 1927 the area is now about 1,100 square miles. The main difficulties had been encountered from mining interests because mining initially appeared to be the only economic advantage that could ever be derived from the territory. That, too, was a big mistake; even in purely economic terms the profit derived from the use of the territory as a park has now grown beyond any imaginable scale.

Until 1901 the South Rim could only be reached by stage coach. Accommodations were primitive, the journey and stay were expensive. But this was more than compensated by the unspoilt natural scenery and the "wild tales" of the pioneers of tourism, such as "Captain" J. Hance and W.W. Bass who gave his name to the Bass limestone. In 1901 the first train from Williams steamed into the still existing railroad depot of El Tovar. Travel costs from Williams to the canyon immediately dropped to one-tenth of the former figure. Soon Fred Harvey, who was responsible for food and accommodations along the Santa Fe Railroad, made provision for the ever-growing number of visitors also on this branch line and at El Tovar. In 1902 the first tourist arrived in his own automobile and "progress" has been irresistible since.

69

In 1905 the El Tovar Hotel was built. In his extremely informative book "The Story of Man at Grand Canyon" (1967) J.D. Hughes reports that a certain Charles F. Whittlesey was commissioned to build a first-class hotel of 100 rooms, "which would combine the architecture of the 'Swiss chateaux' with that of the 'castles of the Rhine' in native boulders, Oregon pine logs and boards".

The El Tovar Hotel was named after that Spaniard who was the first man to visit the pueblos of the Hopi Indians but who never was at Grand Canyon. It shows to this day that Charles F. Whittlesey discharged his task superbly—even though somewhere along the line there was clearly some confusion between a Swiss chalet and a Swiss château.

At any rate, the visitors began to pour in. The figures kept rising, and are still rising, and showed a decline only during the depression of the 30s and during World War II. In 1919 the total was 44,000, in 1923 it was over 100,000, in 1935 over 200,000, in 1941 it was 440,000, in 1944 it had dropped to 65,000 but in 1947 it exceeded 600,000 and in 1963 had reached 1,500,000. Provision of additional accommodations including those of a simpler kind and of camping sites, became necessary. They are all more or less hidden in the forest and in no way disturb the scenery. Roads were built for motorists and picturesque trails laid out. The Canyon Rim Nature Trail, a walk a mile and a quarter long, leads close to the precipice from El Tovar to Yavapai Point. Notice boards planted along it not only explain the view, the plants and the animals, etc., but also stimulate contemplation by appropriate texts. Anyone over 12 years old and weighing less than 200 pounds (including his full equipment) can—provided written notice is given in advance to Fred

Harvey—undertake a two-day tour on muleback down into the

canyon to spend a night at Phantom Ranch at the exit of Bright Angel Canyon, facilities including a swimming pool. There are plans afoot now to develop the locality of Grand Canyon also during the winter months, the dead season, by making it a center for conventions and congresses. From a nearby small airfield the Grand Canyon Airways operates flights over and into the canyon. Bus excursions into the surroundings, Indian dances and camp fire sing-songs, museums and instructional lectures—in short anything that belongs to a highly developed tourist center is now available. Grand Canyon National Park has become big business, a first-class tourist attraction. For those people who desire a silent dialogue with nature the canyon is still the same as ever. But the motivation which brings visitors here has, generally speaking, changed: people are looking for something different and face the landscape in a different manner from former days.

Hand in hand with the opening up of the area to tourism scientific investigation also progressed. In 1902 F.E. Matthes started on a survey and the drawing of a detailed topographical map. The principal sheets of this were available by 1905 but the work as a whole was not completed until 1920 to 1923. We have already mentioned the new geological map by J.H. Maxson (1968). Particular attention has been given to the training of the naturalists who now introduce some hundreds of thousands of listeners to the geology and origins of the area. The effect of their work on people who come from the great cities and are here so impressively confronted with nature is almost impossible to assess.

For a long time an adequate water supply was a particular problem. As recently as 1932 water was brought up in cisterns by the railroad. Now it is being pumped up from a spring deep down in the

canyon (Indian Creek, Indian Gardens).

The Park territory has not so far been extended upstream. On the other hand a large directly adjoining area was added to it in 1932 as the Grand Canyon National Monument. This territory of roughly 300 square miles includes the volcanic phenomena of Toroweap Canyon which we mentioned earlier. Further downstream a special recreational zone was hived off—the Lake Mead Recreational Area which includes Lake Mead with its banks and which extends to Davis Dam. In this way a 250-mile long strip was created along the Colorado River, available to man for recreation and instruction, an area where nature, too, though to a varying degree, enjoys care and protection.

Hans Boesch

Brief captions

1 Dawn over the Grand Canyon
2 The Grand Canyon seen from the North Rim
3 Navajo shepherds in Monument Valley
4 Monument Valley
5 The Grand Canyon seen from Pima Point on the South Rim
6 Navajo shepherds with flock
7 Navajo shepherd
8 Monument Valley
9 Navajo women weaving carpets
10 Montezuma Castle
11 Painted Desert
12, 13 Painted Desert, details
14 "The Big Eye" in Monument Valley
15 Spider Rock in the Canyon de Chelly

16 Petrified tree trunk
17–19 Petrified forest, details
20 Tumbleweed
21 Yucca
22–23 Dead pines
24 Weathered trunk of pinyon pine (Pinus edulis)
25 A giant saguaro
26 Saguaro in flower

1

12

13

15

16

17

18

19

20

22

23

24

25

# Botany

According to A.W. Kuchler's recent mapping of the Potential Natural Vegetation of the Conterminous United States, the vegetation of the Grand Canyon region falls under three general categories: 1. the spruce-fir-Douglas-fir forest—an "open to dense forest of low to medium tall needleleaf evergreen trees with an admixture of broadleaf deciduous low trees and shrubs. The dominant trees are white fir *(Abies concolor)*, Colorado blue spruce *(Picea pungens)*, and Douglas fir *(Pseudotsuga menziesii)*"; 2. the Arizona pine forest—an "open to dense forest of needleleaf evergreen trees, medium tall or tall, frequently with an herbaceous ground cover, the dominant tree being ponderosa pine *(Pinus ponderosa)*"; 3. the juniper-pinyon woodland—consisting of "open groves of needleleaf evergreen low trees with varying admixtures of shrubs and herbaceous plants, the dominant trees being Utah juniper *(Juniperus osteosperma)* and pinyon pine *(Pinus edulis)*". Encroaching on the region along valleys of lower elevations to the west are smaller segments of several additional elements belonging to the "cold-desert" flora of the Great Basin, the Chihuahuan grassland flora of northern Mexico, and the Sonoran desert flora of southwestern Arizona, Nevada and California. Because of the extreme topographic relief of the canyon and the great range of altitudes from the top to the bottom, the vegetation presents a very complex mosaic of these elements, some of which are separated by only a small horizontal space on the map but by hundreds of meters of altitude.

*Descriptive.* Tourists who see the canyon from only the South or the North Rim can hardly say that they have truly seen it, for from the standpoint of the vegetation the two rims of the canyon are different worlds. Gazing from one rim to the other, one can hardly appreciate the great difference in altitude between them, and although one can see from a distance that the North Rim is forested, a revelation awaits those who take the time to see the canyon from the north as well as the south edge.

The South Rim supports an open steppe community dominated by pinyon pine and Utah juniper with a sparse understory of xerophytic shrubs and little grass. There is not much herbaceous vegetation, most of the species having relatively short blossoming seasons. The soil is red, sandy, or clayey, relatively thin and characteristically developing a peculiar crust held together by various species of soil lichens—black, gray, and reddish-brown—which to the untrained eye might appear to be pebbles. The air is aromatic from the resinous exudations of the pine, juniper, sagebrush *(Artemisia),* fern-bush *(Chamaebatiaria millefolium),* bitterbrush *(Purshia)* and cliff-rose *(Cowania).* Even the cacti emit a characteristic but indescribable odor to the melange.

The vegetation of the North Rim or Kaibab Plateau can hardly be compared with that of the South Rim, for the North Rim is much higher in altitude and its vegetation is typically montane. The North Rim in its highest parts is dominated by a forest containing aspen *(Populus tremuloides).* Sloping down toward the north along the stream drainages are numerous moist grassy meadows lined with Colorado blue spruce *(Picea pungens)* and containing scattered ponds. Because of the severe over-browsing by deer which occurred during the years 1906 to 1924, much of the original understory was destroyed and has not recovered. In its place are thickets of weedy shrubs, notably the pink locust *(Robinia neomexicana),* which are of little browse value. The dense forests of the North Rim come abruptly to the canyon wall and with little transition give way to the vegetation of the cliffs.

98 Between the essentially Rocky Mountain forest flora of the North

Rim and the steppe-desert flora of the South Rim we have the complex floristic mosaic of the extremely dissected canyon itself with all of its varied exposures, rock types, shade and moisture conditions. Much of this region, of course, is practically inaccessible to the botanist and little known in detail.

The vegetation of the canyon walls consists of herbs and shrubs that are able to germinate and survive in the rock crevices themselves (chasmophytes) or plants that can cling to the rapidly eroding summits of pinnacles and arete-like erosion features. Such plants as scrub oak *(Quercus gambelii)*, mountain mahogany *(Cercocarpus intricatus)* and cliff-rose *(Cowania mexicana)* form impenetrable thickets on steep slopes. The rare and unusual silk-tassel bush *(Garrya wrightii)* occurs just below the North Rim Lodge along a cliff-side trail. In cooler sites occasional small stands of Douglas fir and big-tooth maple *(Acer grandidentatum)* fill alcoves in the canyon walls.

The vegetation of the canyon-bottom itself is conditioned by the flow of the river and by the availability of suitable sites. On the side of the canyon that is continually scoured by running water, there are smooth massive sandstone walls where no plants can gain a foothold. Occasionally these walls are streaked by dark "flow-lines" of lichens *(Staurothele* and *Verrucaria)* that colonize surfaces periodically moistened by seepage water coming down from above. Sand-bars periodically flooded are colonized by phreatophytic shrubs such as tamarisk *(Tamarix pentandra)*, an adventive from southwest Asia, species of willow (*Salix exigua* and others) cottonwood *(Populus fremontii)*, and in late summer by a host of weedy herbs such as cocklebur *(Xanthium strumarium)*, wild licorice *(Glycyrrhiza lepidota)*, seep-willow *(Baccharis glutinosa)*, and giant reeds *(Phragmites australis)*. The plants of the canyon walls also reach the riverside where the talus slopes of box canyons, alluvial fans or similar outwash deposits support sagebrush and rabbit-brush communities on river benches.

*Historical Phytogeography.* From the point of view of historical phytogeography, the flora of the Grand Canyon belongs to at least three important elements: the Cordilleran Forest Province, the Colorado Plateaus Province, and the Sonoran Province. The highlands of the North Rim are clothed with the southernmost forests of the Cordilleran Forest Province; and although there is no altitude in the National Park high enough to support an alpine tundra flora, the San Francisco Peaks, just to the south, have on their summits the ultimate extension of the alpine tundra of the northern Cordillera in the United States.

In any region where the landscape is monotonous, the relief slight, and the flora homogeneous, a major climatic shift or environmental catastrophe may completely exterminate a vegetation type and permit it to be entirely replaced by new invaders. Thus in some areas of the world, major climatic shifts or orogenic movements can profoundly alter the vegetation, the Continental glaciations of the Pleistocene affording a prime example.

However, in a region of extreme relief and great range in altitude such as the Grand Canyon, it is possible for species to survive drastic climatic changes by making short migrations upward or downward or simply by being preserved in a specific habitat with a microclimate that remains intact through being buffered by its surroundings. One might look at the Grand Canyon Flora as containing survivors in some small degree from all of the floras which have inhabited it since its availability to colonization by land plants.

The Grand Canyon lies within the Colorado Plateaus Physiographic Province, which as a unit has been available to land plants since the Cretaceous Period and has not been directly affected by continental glaciation or by its related pluvial periods. Certainly the Colorado Plateaus area is an important reservoir for survivors of the Tertiary flora. Moreover, its lithological and altitudinal diversity and its aridity has provided a rich laboratory for the evolution of numerous endemic species.

The Sonoran element, if it can be said to belong to the Grand Canyon, enters the area only in the very westernmost part and only a few of its representatives, such as the ocotillo *(Fouquieria splendens)* and creosote bush *(Larrea tridentata)* reach the borders of the National Park. These plants, along with the giant saguaro cactus *(Carnegiea gigantea),* inhabit the hot deserts of southern Arizona. It would appear that the Sonoran element has begun to penetrate the Grand Canyon region only in post-Pleistocene time.

Among the "living fossils" that grow in the Grand Canyon region are the joint firs *(Ephedra)* which must have been abundant during the Tertiary in Eurasia and America but are now restricted to comparatively small areas, the Arizona walnut *(Juglans major),* mulberry *(Morus microphylla),* three species of holly-grape *(Mahonia),* *Crossosoma parviflorum,* the hop-tree *(Ptelea trifoliata),* the bigtooth maple *(Acer grandidentatum), Ayenia* in the Sterculiaceae and species of *Garrya* in the Garryaceae. Several of these genera occur as fossils in the Tertiary deposits of western United States. The bristlecone pine *(Pinus aristata)* which still grows on the San Francisco Peaks, is known from excellently preserved fossils of needles and cones from the Oligocene beds of southern Colorado.

Although the Colorado Plateaus have been available to habitation by land plants for an extraordinarily long period of time, the cutting

of the canyon itself is a relatively recent event, beginning probably in the Middle Pliocene, about nine million years ago. Has the canyon itself since that time become an important barrier to the movement of the flora; and has it, during that time, through the inevitable isolation of segments of existing populations, been instrumental in the development of discrete races?

Among the mammals, the Kaibab squirrel has evolved distinct races separated by the canyon barriers. Among the plants, however, we still know too little in detail about the species to know whether this has occurred with any frequency. One clear example, however, is the desert sunflower *(Wyethia scabra),* which consists of three distinct taxonomic races, one restricted to sandy areas north of the Colorado River, a second south of the Grand Canyon, and a third in the region east of the Green River. These races in all probability were established as a result of their isolation effected by the down-cutting of the Grand Canyon.

*Evolution.* The Grand Canyon is actually and potentially a great natural laboratory for the testing of new plant genotypes and thus for the evolution of new species. This is because the region combines an enormous range of altitude with a great variety of exposures to the sun and the weather, but especially because the prevailing climate is arid. G.L. Stebbins analyzed this phenomenon in 1952 in a paper entitled "Aridity as a Stimulus to Plant Evolution". Citing G.G. Simpson's observation that the relatively static populations of plants have nearly all existed in environments which have remained relatively constant and continuously favorable, he added the obverse, namely that "the most rapid evolution would occur in habitats which are changing, and in particular those which are limiting or deficient in some factor essential to the existence of the organism". He gives three reasons why evolution should be rela-

102

tively rapid in arid or semi-arid regions: 1. Where moisture is a limiting factor, local diversity in topography, soil, and other factors will have a much greater effect on the character of the vegetation than in regions where moisture is adequate; 2. population structure of the component species is likely to be particularly favorable (populations tend to be smaller because their habitats are smaller, flowering times are shorter and the open habitat tends to favor annual forms); and 3. in arid regions there is a great opportunity for a variety of different specialized structures to develop, which plants can evolve for adaptation to dry conditions (reduction of leaf surface, development of trichomes, scales and other coverings, sunken stomata, caducous leaves, extensive and deep root systems, bulbs, storage roots or adaptation of the cell sap itself to withstand prolonged drought, as in the bryophytes).

*Endemism.* Although the Colorado Plateaus area as a whole is rich in endemic species, relatively few species are limited to the region of the Grand Canyon itself. Most of the common habitats for plants are widespread throughout the plateau region, and the Grand Canyon has few habitats which are unique to itself. However, the general absence of moist habitats in the region suggests that the springs and sites of water seepage over rocks, few and isolated as they are, might be potential areas for narrowly restricted endemic species. And this is quite true. The canyons are noted for their rare "hanging gardens"—moist ledges on the canyon walls that are wet by spray from small waterfalls or by water seeping from springs or through the joints in the rocks. The hanging gardens are virtual oases on the sheer cliffs of the canyons and support some of the most exciting endemic species, among which are the handsome

103  pink-flowered *Primula hunnewellii* and the sedge, *Carex curatorum.*

Other, not strictly endemic, forms are the red monkey-flower *(Mimulus cardinalis),* the orchid *Epipactis gigantea,* and the venus-hair fern *(Adiantum capillus-veneris).*

*The March of the Seasons.* The best wild-flower displays occur too early or too late in the year to be seen by most tourists, and often several years go by without a good display because of the erratic pattern of annual precipitation. In the pinyon-juniper and sagebrush areas of the South Rim the early spring wild flowers appear in April and May. Many of them are short-lived annuals or biennials with only a few weeks of active growth before they disappear with the onset of summer. These delicate and ephemeral plants belong predominantly to the mustard (Cruciferae), phlox (Polemoniaceae), knotweed (Polygonaceae), borage (Boraginaceae) and daisy (Compositae) families. Winter rains are important for a good flowering season.

A few perennials, such as the low growing *Pedicularis centranthera,* blossom as soon as the snow melts but they complete their flowering so soon that few people see anything but the leaves, which mature later on. In areas where the sedimentary rock formations are turned steeply on edge and several distinctly different substrates are in close contact yet do not contaminate each other by their erosion products, very rich assemblages of ephemeral early spring-flowering species occur following good winter rains. Among these are a number of genera which apparently are able to tolerate unusually high concentrations of toxic elements such as selenium *(Stanleya, Astragalus)* or which are limited to areas of high concentrations of gypsum *(Frankenia* and some species of *Eriogonum).* When these plants are in blossom, huge expanses of extremely barren clay may be transformed for a few days into golden, pink, or white carpets through the massing of thousands of minute blossoms.

Late spring and early summer is the time of flowering of the shrubby plants of the South Rim, many of which belong to the Rosaceae. Those most characteristic of the area have small, xeromorphic, glutinous leaves and often have conspicuous white or yellow flowers. Bitterbrush, cliff-rose and fernbush are abundant along the rim. Several of these rosaceous shrubs are more conspicuous in fruit than in flower, for their mature fruits develop beautiful elongated plumose styles. Apache plume *(Fallugia paradoxa)* and the mountain mahoganies *(Cercocarpus intricatus, C. ledifolius,* and *C. montanus)* are good examples of this. One of the most unusual of the shrubs is the rock-mat *(Petrophytum caespitosum)* a close relative of *Spiraea,* which grows in dense mats on cliff faces. Its stems are only a half-inch high, with rosettes of stiff blunt leaves and short spikes of white flowers.

Late summer brings a profusion of blossoming in the sagebrushes *(Artemisia),* shrubby *Eriogonum* and rabbit-brush *(Chrysothamnus).* The American sagebrushes should not be confused with the culinary sage *(Salvia)* or the "purple sage" *(Salvia dorrii)* of Zane Grey's western novel, but they are instead woody *Artemisia* species with highly aromatic leaves. The sagebrush of the rim include a small dark species only a few decimeters tall *(Artemisia nova)* and a low silvery species *(A. bigelovii)* while the species in the deeper soils of the canyon bottoms and "arroyos" is a gray plant *(A. tridentata)* often attaining a height of ten feet. Rabbit-brush *(Chrysothamnus nauseosus)* displays large round-topped corymbs of bright yellow flower heads contrasting elegantly with the linear silver-gray leaves and stems.

Autumnal coloration seldom appears before the end of the tourist season, but in late August the South Rim is brightened by the coloring of the many kinds of shrubs, the scrub oak *(Quercus)* and serviceberry *(Amelanchier)*. A special thrill awaits the visitor to the North Rim in early September, where at the much higher altitude he is able to watch the gradual changes in coloration of the aspen, and to see the big-tooth maple paint small alcoves in the canyon walls a brilliant salmon pink or deeper crimson. The contrasting colors of the yellow aspen leaves against the deep green needles of the Colorado blue spruce and the blue sky vie in beauty with the ever-changing colors of the canyon itself.

Edible fruits are not abundant in the Grand Canyon area. Although some species undoubtedly were used by the Indians, those that are available are neither abundant enough nor suitable for civilized man's tastes. Red raspberry *(Rubus idaeus),* choke cherry *(Prunus virginiana)* Oregon-grape *(Mahonia repens),* canyon grape *(Vitis arizonica)* and several kinds of currants and gooseberries *(Ribes)* are among the most common species.

Although one thinks of botanical attractions chiefly as blossom-time events, the Grand Canyon region at any season displays interesting botanical phenomena for the observant visitor. After the flowering period is quite finished, many of the plants then are faced with the problem of dispersing their seeds over the large areas of vacant land available to them. With the inability of the arid landscape to support dense, closed stands of plants, an advantage is conferred on those species that are adapted for long distance dispersal. One of the methods characteristic of the arid steppe species is the "tumbleweed" habit. Tumbleweeds do not easily shed their seeds, but instead the entire plant, stems, seeds and all, develop a globular habitus that permits them to roll along the ground, tumbling over and over. As they tumble, small bits of the branches break off, so that individual seeds are detached along with the

twigs as the parent plant continues its hegira. The characteristic tumbleweeds of the region belong to the Chenopodiaceae (*Salsola, Corispermum* and *Cycloloma*) but several species of *Eriogonum* produce inflated stems or diffuse, finely divided inflorescences that create aerodynamic dispersal mechanisms. Tumbleweeds carried across the steppe by the strong winter winds or sandstorms are the essence of off-season Grand Canyon botany.


*Parasites and Saprophytes.* Among the Grand Canyon plants, some of the most interesting are the parasites and saprophytes. The juniper *(Juniperus osteosperma)* for example, is commonly attacked by a parasitic mistletoe *(Phoradendron juniperinum)* whose growth habit mimics the appearance of its host, just as in Australia the various species of mistletoe *(Amyema)* mimic the species of *Eucalyptus* and *Casuarina* on which they occur. The parasitic flowering plants of the pinyon-juniper forest include several kinds of broom-rape *(Orobanche)* that are parasitic on the roots of other plants, notably *Artemisia.* The deserts of Southwestern United States are a center of diversity for this group as are the deserts of North Africa. The orchid *Corallorhiza* and the pinedrops *(Pterospora andromedea)* grow in the litter at the base of pine trees. The latter is commonly mistaken for *Corallorhiza* but is a leafless member of the heath family (Ericaceae).

If one is unfamiliar with desert regions at all seasons, it is a distinct surprise to discover that distinctive forms of mushrooms are to be found here. There are the stalked puffballs *(Tylostoma),* gasteromycetes in all respects but with a stout and durable stalk. Often the base of the stalk rests on the bedrock, while the puffball is raised to the level of the sandy soil surface, leaving the stalk invisible in the ground. Another stalked puffball *(Battarea diguetii)* inhabits areas of shifting sand. Its stalk is shaggy with loose papery plates, and the

107

puffball is circumscissile, the upper part persisting as a cap over the spore mass. Specimens of *Battarea* often reach two or three decimeters in height. Earth stars *(Geaster)* are also common on the soils of the pinyon-juniper woodland, the woody outer walls of the puffball spreading widely on the ground in the form of a black or gray five-pointed star, with the papery, globose-inflated spore-case lying in the center. One of the strangest of the mushrooms is the gilled mushroom *Montagnites,* because the jet-black gills are naked; that is, they are not covered by the cap that one normally expects to find on the gilled fungi. The stalk is stout and woody, but as might be expected, the gills are extremely fragile and are soon destroyed upon exposure to the elements.

*Succulents.* No account of the plants of Arizona should fail to mention the most characteristic plants of the region—the cacti, the agaves, and the yuccas. Although the altitudes of the Grand Canyon are too high, and the possibility of destructive frosts too obvious, for the great wealth of these plants of the Sonoran element to be well-represented here, a good variety of cacti and succulents can be found. The largest and most conspicuous is the cholla *(Opuntia whipplei)* which belongs to the group of prickly-pear cacti with cylindrical stems forming low, extremely spiny bushes. Each of the principal spines is hooked, and if one falls into a patch, the removal of the plant from the seat of the trousers can be a very painful experience. Several species of the flat-branched *Opuntia* are common in the Canyon, and have blossoms of pink, yellow, or copper-gold. Hedgehog cacti *(Echinocereus)* have barrel-like, short stems usually grouped in massive clusters, and the barrel cacti *(Echinocactus)* usually have solitary barrel-like stems. If the principal spines are hooked such a cactus may be called a "bear claw".

Unfortunately, one cannot see the giant cactus or saguaro *(Carnegiea gigantea),* the night-blooming *Cereus,* or the fantastic "jumping cholla" cacti in the Grand Canyon. These are true representatives of the Sonoran flora and are found only in the southern parts of Arizona.

Several kinds of *Yucca,* or Spanish bayonet, inhabit the pinyon-juniper woodland and canyonsides. The most attractive of these is *Yucca baccata,* whose broad, stout sword-like leaves remind one of some African *Aloë.* In favorable seasons these plants produce enormous clusters of large white pendent flowers. The yucca was one of the most useful of all the plants gathered by the Indians of the area.

Century plants *(Agave)* can be seen clinging to the steep walls of the canyon just below the rim. Their huge rigid leaves, with stout curved prickles along the margins are a formidable protection for the tall candelabra of yellow flowers up to 30 feet tall. The plant uses up a great deal of stored nutriment in producing this fantastic flower display and dies immediately after flowering.

*Poisonous Plants.* The Grand Canyon has no plants that are poisonous to the touch, such as poison ivy *(Toxicodendron),* but some people are subject to a dermatitis if they touch the milky juice exuding from the cut stem of some species of *Euphorbia* which are native here. The Grand Canyon euphorbias are all herbaceous and hardly resemble their cactus-like relatives in North Africa. The bulbous underground stem of the lily, *Zigadenus venenosus* is extremely poisonous and has the local name "death camass". Although humans need not worry about plant poisoning here, several of the native plants are poisonous to livestock. Particularly certain species of the pea family (Leguminosae), the mustard family (Cruciferae) and the daisy family (Compositae) demonstrate selenophily. These plants are not only able to survive on soils that are high in selenium content but they store quantities of selenium in their tissues, which makes the plants poisonous. The crucifer, prince's plume *(Stanleya pinnata)* is a "selenium indicator plant" growing on extremely arid sites, with candle-like racemes of bright yellow flowers. Other plants poisonous to livestock commonly seen in the Grand Canyon are the larkspurs *(Delphinium)* with blue, spurred flowers, and loco weeds *(Oxytropis)* with racemes of deep violet flowers.


*Adventives.* Disturbed soils along roadsides and in camping places, along footpaths and animal trails are colonized by enterprising adventive plants, principally native in southeastern Europe and southwest Asia. This situation is not unique to the Grand Canyon, but quite typical of all North America. In fact, the European flora so dominates the roadside flora that in many parts of the country the tourist from Europe traveling by bus or car, if he cannot see beyond the roadside, might not only recognize many old friends in the roadside flora but remain oblivious to much of the indigenous American flora which lies hidden just beyond. Thus, in America, the common mullein *(Verbascum thapsus)* is everpresent along the roadsides, along with sweet clovers *(Melilotus alba* and *M. officinalis),* and the thistle *(Cirsium arvense).*

Certain indigenous plants are very successful in colonizing the bare ground of roadsides, however, and some of these are beautiful and conspicuous elements of the Grand Canyon flora. The evening primrose *(Oenothera caespitosa),* with its enormous white flowers produced close to the ground in a rosette of leaves, opens early in the morning and later turns pink and withers in the heat of the day.

110 The stickleaf, *Mentzelia rusbyi* (Loasaceae) another morning- and

evening-blossoming species with yellowish-white flowers resembling those of the night-blooming *Cereus* makes showy displays on road-cut-banks.

*Economic Plants.* Before the introduction of maize in about 200–300 A.D., the Navajo and Hopi had been a hunting and gathering people. Maize, beans, and squash came to the Grand Canyon by means of trade and communication with tribes to the south, including Mexico. Even as they adopted the new cultivated crops, the people relied strongly on the wild plants of the region for food, clothing, medicine, and ceremonials.

*Yucca* was probably the most important single plant in the economy of the ancient Indians of the Southwest. Almost every part of the plant was utilized—the buds, flowers, and succulent emerging inflorescences were eaten raw or cooked, the fruits of the pulpy *Yucca baccata* were eaten raw or roasted, dried for winter use or ground into meal. These also provided a fermented mash for an alcoholic drink. The tough fibers from the swordlike leaves were pounded out and separated to make rope, sandals, mats, baskets and cloth. The roots could be used for making soap and had laxative qualities.

The Indians gathered for food the underground parts of sego lilies *(Calochortus),* wild onions *(Allium),* several Umbelliferae including *Cymopterus,* an indigenous but very small-tubered potato *(Solanum jamesii)* and cat-tails *(Typha latifolia).* Many succulent herbs were eaten as we prepare spinach—*Rumex, Chenopodium, Amaranthus* and the young shoots of the bee-plant *(Cleome serrulata).*

Berry crops in the region are unpredictable and the berries are mostly dry and unattractive to modern palates, but the fruits of the
111 cacti, *Amelanchier, Celtis, Prunus,* and *Peraphyllum* were gathered

and ground up to make an edible paste. In bad seasons the people had to rely on the bitter fruits of *Juniperus* and those of the mistletoe, *Phoradendron*. Many kinds of weed and grass seeds were harvested and ground up into a flour, but the most useful of all the seed crops was the pinyon pine which bears seeds heavily in this, its native home. At the present time the pinyon pine is an important export crop among the Indians and the nuts are to be found in shops all over America, competing very successfully with the imported nuts of the Mediterranean *Pinus pinea*.

*Phragmites australis,* locally known as carrizo, was used by the Indians for making arrow-shafts, prayer sticks, weaving rods, pipestems, mats, screens, cordage, nets and thatching. The rhizomes and the seeds were sometimes used as food.

Plants used for making tea included the mistletoe *(Phoradendron)* and the beggar's tick *(Thelesperma)*. Latex-containing species such as the Colorado rubber-plant *(Hymenoxys)*, were chewed as we chew gum, and the indigenous tobacco *(Nicotiana attenuata),* was cultivated for smoking. And for the Indians as for all primitive peoples the indigenous flora furnished an extensive pharmacopeia. Weaving cloth and blankets from wool or cotton was learned by the Pueblo people from tribes in Central America as early as 600 A.D., the Navajo learning the art from the Pueblo. Along with silver craft, rugs and blankets are among the most beautiful handwork of the Navajo. Until recent time, the colors of the wool were all produced from dyes obtained from native plants. The dyeing technique was evolved long before cotton and wool became available and in ancient times was applied to articles fashioned from yucca fiber. Since 1880, the analine dyes have largely replaced native plants. Among the plant products used for mordants in dyeing, tannic acid was obtained from sumac *(Rhus trilobata)*, dock *(Rumex hymenosepalus),* and gum from the pinyon pine. The roots of *Cercocar-*

*pus* yielded a red-brown dye, *Chrysothamnus* blossoms a golden yellow, and *Rumex hymenosepalus* a rich brown and a gold. Red, blue and purple colors were obtained from sunflower *(Helianthus)*, and from maize. The ancient dye process is a very complicated subject and a thorough study of it has only recently been undertaken. Fortunately, many of the old recipes are still known to the elders of the tribes, and curiosity among Americans in the ancient techniques are reviving the art among hobbyists as well as anthropologists.

*Mosses and Lichens.* One would expect mosses to be extremely rare in such an arid environment as the Grand Canyon. Nevertheless, if one is observant there is really no dearth of them. Wherever a small patch of snow lies beneath the shaded side of a small shrub there will be a corresponding colony of the ever-present desert soil moss, *Tortula ruralis* or, in more xeric sites, its miniature relative, *Tortula bistratosa,* a much smaller plant that compensates for the smaller surface area of its leaves by increasing its effective photosynthetic material by a doubled layer of leaf cells. Other desert mosses in the Grand Canyon area show comparable modifications. Another common small soil moss is *Pterygoneurum.* In dry weather its leaves are closely imbricate, but when wet they spread apart and expose vertical plates of green cells arising from the midrib. A third is *Crossidium,* occupying crevices of the cliffs. The upper side of the leaf is so thickly studded with erect green filaments that, when wet, it resembles a small hairbrush. In these various ways the desert mosses, by packing an extraordinary amount of photosynthetic material into the smallest possible space, can take advantage of brief and infrequent periods of humidity. In the dry state, the mosses have a charred, black and dead appearance, but when the air becomes ever so slightly humid they expand in a few moments into beautiful green cushions.

Of the three principal growth forms of lichens, the fruticose type is extremely rare. There are virtually no fruticose species growing on the ground, and the fruticose growth form on trees is represented only by *Usnea,* the beard lichen. Even this is rare except in the spruce-fir forests. Wherever *Usnea* occurs it is an indication of locally high humidity. The highly restricted occurrence of *Usnea,* even in places where one might expect it to occur, may be correlated with late-lying snow-patches under the trees, where a small area of *Usnea* may be present on tree branches directly overhanging the snow-patch, where the evaporation of the snow temporarily saturates the area above the ground level.

In the pinyon-juniper woodland, foliose lichens are sometimes conspicuous on the tree trunks. Most of these belong to the genus *Parmelia,* of which one of the most common species is the large green rosette-forming *Parmelia flaventior.* Another very common yellow-green species, *Parmelia chlorochroa,* grows unattached to any substrate and drifts like a tumbleweed into little heaps on the ground between clumps of grass and sagebrush. It apparently obtains what small amounts of inorganic nutrients it needs from the dust particles precipitated by humid air. This lichen occasionally accumulates in large quantities in wind-rows, and is one of the important ingredients of the wool-dyeing processes used by the Navajo.

The crustose lichens dominate the inhospitably arid substrates of soil and rock in the Grand Canyon, and since many of them are strikingly colored red, orange, yellow, green, white and black, they are responsible for much of the secondary colorations of the rocks. In fact, many tourists never learn that these are in fact plants and not parts of the rocks themselves.

The crustose lichens owe their success to several inherent qualities. They are, for the most part, very slow-growing (a plaque of *Rhizocarpon,* nine inches in diameter, in Colorado has been reliably estimated as being very close to 6,000 years old). They are able to tolerate long and severe periods of drought and desiccation without being killed, and by their power of almost instantaneous absorption of water from humid air they can take advantage of extremely short periods of time that are favorable for growth. They grow so slowly that they neither outgrow their substrate nor do they break down the rock sufficiently to produce much soil which would permit their competitors, the higher plants, to replace them. The lichen combination, furthermore, permits the two symbionts, the fungus thallus and the algal cells which it envelops, to co-exist on a forbidding substrate on which neither partner could possibly exist on its own.

The mosses and lichens, probably more than the flowering plants in this region, show distinct preferences for acidic or for calcareous or nitrophious substrates. The lichens probably show these tendencies most dramatically. In the northern world, especially in the oceanic climates, where high amount of rainfall rapidly leach out nitrogenous material, a characteristic phenomenon is that of the "birdrock" or "Vogeltopp" lichen, usually the brilliant orange *Xanthoria parietina* which colors the rocks inhabited by sea birds. These nitrophilous lichen colonies are visible for long distances and completely cover large areas of rocks. Orange lichens of this genus are also common on trees bordering dusty lanes or roads along which horses and other livestock move.

In the desert and steppe the leaching effect of precipitation is minimal, and the nitrogenous waste products of animals are extremely long-lasting. Along dusty sheep trails, particularly in areas that may be flooded in spring, the bare woody trunks of the sagebrush and greasewood bushes are frequently completely covered by species of *Xanthoria fallax* or *X. polycarpa.* Where vegetation is lacking, however, the presence of nitrogenous wastes may be traced by dry orange "waterfalls" of lichens of the genus *Caloplaca* "flowing" down a cliff face or from the summit of a boulder used by a hunting bird. Sometimes these highly colored "flow lines" lead upward to small depressions containing a few rodent feces or a often used rodent urinal marked by a patch of white precipitate.

Thus one finds that the most conspicuous element of the lichen flora of the canyon is the nitrophilous *Caloplaca* group. Vertical rock faces (and *only* vertical faces) are often colored a bright chartreuse-green by *Acarospora chlorophana,* while horizontal ones have smaller colonies of its close relative *A. schleicheri.* The lichens have extraordinary qualities of absorption, and many of the desert species are able to extract calcium from the substrate and precipitate it on the lichen surface as calcium oxalate, giving the lichen itself a chalk-white appearance. This phenomenon is matched in the subarctic where some species take iron from the substrate and precipitate it as iron oxide, giving the lichen a rust-colored surface. The crustose lichens are exceedingly slow-growing and endure for centuries or, in some well-documented instances, millenia. Over these extremely long periods the plants are exposed to extremes of heat, cold, drought, abrasion by wind and sand blasts, and they themselves through chemical weathering cause exfoliation of the rock on which they grow. Through all of this attrition the lichens frequently are much altered in appearance and present special problems in identification and interpretation.

*Soil Crust.* A characteristic if not unique feature of the pinyon-juniper woodland and the adjacent sagebrush steppe is the presence of a well-developed and fragile soil crust. We do not know much about the genesis of this crust, but the silty soils that overlie the sandstone or limestone bedrocks would be washed away very quickly by the violent torrential showers which are so characteristic of the region if it were not for the fact that the surface is bound together by the thalli of cryptogamic plants. The first colonists of the soil surface are species of blue-green algae, and these are soon joined or replaced by a number of crustose lichens, whose thalli are shield-like plates from the undersides of which slender hyphae or fungal threads penetrate and interlace through the upper levels of the soil. *Collema coccophorum,* for example, is a black lichen whose algal component is *Nostoc. Lecidea decipiens* is a brick-red crust with black globose apothecia on the margins of the saucer-shaped thallus. *Dermatocarpon lachneum* is a cervine-brown species with the fruiting bodies immersed in the crust and visible only as minute black pinpricks on the surface. These lichens not only bind the soil but their capacity to absorb moisture in great quantities and to form swollen cushions serves to soften the impact of raindrops and thus to make the soil crust resistant to raindrop erosion. This is quite apparent where the crust is not complete, and erosion between crusts results in a series of pedestals of soil capped by lichens, with eroded channels between them.

In the wintertime these soil crusts, with the moisture that is retained in the soil by the lichen crusts on the surface, are profoundly affected by the formation of needle ice, which raises the upper level of the crust above the deeper soil layers, with the result that the crust becomes like the layer of thin ice in a small pond, easily broken through by the pressure of a foot. When one walks through an area of soil crust, one is conscious of the crust collapsing beneath him, and looking back, he can see the footprints depressed to the depth of several centimeters.

The breaking of the soil crust on a large scale often does irreparable damage to the vegetation. This is easily seen when a public campground is established in a pinyon-juniper woodland with a well-developed soil crust. The breaking of the soil crust by the footsteps of man replaces a crusted soil surface, that up to this time was resistant to wind or water erosion, with a loose, silty surface. Before the soil crust has an opportunity to be rebuilt, the area is invaded by the Eurasian weed flora which perhaps was not a factor before the advent of western man. The locality soon becomes a waste area which, for a short time each spring, may be populated with a dense cover of cheat grass *(Bromus tectorum)*. This soon dries up, leaving no protection against the wind and the rain, and soon the thin layer of soil, perhaps only a few centimeters deep, has blown away, leaving only the sandstone bedrock. The area may commonly be further denuded by the campers themselves, who, in attempting to find convenient places for their tents, remove not only the loose stones lying about, but remove every cactus, sagebrush, or other shrub which would interfere with their floor. In one national monument, the writer knows of such a campground that was established in one of the most scenic areas. When the original site was effectively destroyed, the Park administration decided to let the campground recover, so they closed this area and established another campground close by in the same scenic area. Instead of recovering, these ruined sites will continue to show the signs of man for generations, and the new campgrounds will deteriorate quickly in the same manner, until eventually, the native vegetation of the entire area is destroyed. Unfortunately, no research has been done to determine the conditions under which a soil crust forms, or just how long a time is needed. Soil crust of this kind, once destroyed, may, in fact, take decades to recover.

William A. Weber

118

Brief captions

27 Desert View Observation Tower, Desert View Point, South Rim

28 Northern part of Havasu Canyon

29 Pinyon pine *(Pinus edulis)* on the South Rim

30 View from Bright Angel Point, North Rim

31 Kanab Canyon, North Rim

32 View from Yaki Point, South Rim

33 The Colorado, seen from Toroweap Point

34 Rock alcove on the South Rim

35 The Colorado near Lava Falls

36 The boats which took us down the Colorado

37 Jean Heiniger

38, 40 Driftwood

39 The botanist

41 Ernst A. Heiniger

42 Our rafts being made fast

43 Parched river bank along the Colorado

44 Tamarisks on the river bank

45 Our rafts "riding at anchor"

46 Foaming waves in the muddy Colorado

47 The Colorado

48 Willow on the river bank

49 The Canyon's rock wall

50 Cavernous alcove in the canyon wall

51 *Yucca elata* on the bank of the Colorado

52 Flowering tamarisk

53 Cliffs in the Toroweap area

54 "Architectural" shapes on the cliff face

55 Horizontal rock strata

56 Folded strata

57 Waterfall into the Colorado

58 The Toroweap lava stream

59 Ocotillo

60 Canyon wall polished by high water

61 Sand trickling down the scarp

62 Eroded sand banks

63 Ocotillo, with the Colorado in the background

64 Inflorescences of ocotillo

65 Sandstone cliffs with rock-mat

66 Vegetation on the canyon floor

67 Flowering mallows on the Colorado's bank

68 Common sotol and ocotillo

69 Elves Chasm

70, 71 Elves Chasm, details

72 Old man prickly pear

73 Hedgehog cactus

74 Grizzly bear cactus (right) and barrel cacti

75 *Opuntia violacea*

76 Barrel cactus

77 Buckhorn cholla

31

37

38

39

40

41

42

43

44

45

46

50

56

57

61

65

67

68

70

71

73

74

75

76

## Fauna

It is only to be expected that a majestic landscape such as the Grand Canyon must also be inhabited by a magnificent fauna. All kinds of superlatives have been used to describe this habitat: the label "gorge of gorges" is only one of many attempts to convey the overwhelming impression produced by these "inverted mountains" on man when he steps up to the gigantic precipice.

Yet the term "inverted mountains", a range which does not tower skyward but downward to vertiginous depths, is something more than a reflection of our inhability to find words for this unparalleled natural phenomenon. For here, too, there is a stratification which largely determines the occurrence of plants and animals. We have here similar changes of atmospheric pressure according to altitude above sea level, of soil and air humidity, air currents, radiation, temperature, etc. Added to these ecological factors there are topographical ones and others. Not all creatures are climbers; certain animals and plants prefer level ground and avoid steep slopes.

But the reader of this book will not expect to find in the chapter on animals a lot of figures about the ecological or zoo-geographical peculiarities of the Grand Canyon but rather a survey of some of the principal animals living in this unique habitat, the species that may be encountered by the tourist who treats himself to the unforgettable experience of riding down on muleback into these colorful fascinating depths.

Such an informal treatment also relieves us of the obligation of considering the animals in these splendid pictures in anything like the order of a zoological textbook. Instead we shall start with the real "ruler" of this truly fantastic landscape—the mountain lion or, as he is usually called in Europe, the puma.

Except for the jaguar the mountain lion is the largest cat of the

North American continent; it goes by several other names, such as cougar, catamount or even panther. The Spaniards called it León Americanol. Zoologically the mountain lion has nothing to do with the big cats of the Old World, such as the lion or the panther, i.e. it differs form them as much as it differs from the small cats, and zoologists in consequence experience considerable difficulty in accommodating it in the system of cats. The question is whether the mountain lion, which can reach a weight of more than 220 pounds, should be included in the species *Panthera,* to which lion, tiger, leopard, jaguar and others belong, or whether it should be included with the small cats in the species *Felis.* An argument in favor of the latter solution is the strange circumstance that mountain lions purr like domestic cats; yet their size is more in line with the leopard, lion, tiger, etc., i.e. the so-called roaring cats. Jn an attempt to find a way out of this embarrassment the mountain lion has been described as a giant small cat but this sounds about as odd as a reference to dwarf giant snakes. A more logical solution is the inclusion of the mountain lion in a new group of so-called medium cats with the scientific name *Puma concolor.*

We may safely leave the intricacies of systematic zoology to the experts, some of whom have distinguished about 30 different races of mountain lion and others as many as over a hundred. Three of these have been found in the Grand Canyon where a lively immigration of mountain lions from Mexico can be observed because the numerous deer continually attract more of the predators. One result, admittedly, has also been the fact that, within the framework of so-called game management, many mountain lions have been officially shot in the state of Arizona because, in the opinion of experts, they decimate the stock of deer and make intolerable inroads on domestic livestock—not only sheep and goats, pigs and calves, but occasionally even horses.

In very exceptional cases mountain lions have even been reported to have attacked humans. Thus S.P. Young and E.A. Goldman, in their monograph on the mountain lion, published in 1946, record that a boy of 13, while walking from one farm to another, was attacked and partially devoured by a mountain lion. Admittedly this tragic incident happened a long time ago, in 1924, and occurred not at the Grand Canyon but in the state of Washington.

The mountain lion has—or rather had—an enormous geographical distribution, extending from Canada to Patagonia and embracing altitudes from sea level to over 13,000 feet. It is the most widespread of all American mammals in the double continent.

No other attacks on humans are known from our own century in which the mountain lion, like most wild beasts, has been increasingly forced back and locally even exterminated. On the other hand, it is worth reporting that mountain lions are quite often eaten by humans. Such gourmets cannot quite agree on whether roast mountain lion is more like chicken or veal. They praise in particular the taste and tenderness of young animals which still bear the juvenile spotted fur. Naturally it is the skin of the mountain lion that is chiefly in demand; this can display various shades ranging from grey to reddish and is marked by exceptional toughness. It is even claimed that dogs find it difficult to bite through its skin. Because of this enormous toughness the skin was frequently used in the pioneering days for the manufacture of shoes and, of course, saddle cloths, cloaks, etc. The hair was a suitable raw material for painter's brushes and the claws and skulls were used by the Indians in the old days for the manufacture of various kinds of personal adornment and ceremonial instruments. This magnificent big cat is now threatened by technology everywhere, but a mere hundred years ago it caused a lot of trouble to settlers by attacking their livestock.

Thus the well-known Swiss naturalist, doctor and diplomat Johann Jakob von Tschudi from Glarus, who after taking his doctor's degree in Zurich engaged in extensive expeditions in mountain lion territories, has this to report in his "Travels Through South America" ("Reisen durch Südamerika", Brockhaus 1869). "After midnight we were awakened by a wild stampede of the flock and by furious barking of dogs, and it took a long time for the animals to calm down again. In the morning it emerged that an impertinent mountain lion had picked himself a sheep from the flock and had escaped with it across a five-foot boarded fence. This was a cheeky predator, used to human habitations. Our landlord complained that this beast of prey had already abducted a few dozen of his sheep and that in spite of all caution, in spite of dogs, lookouts, traps and hunts it had not yet been possible to catch it." The mountain lion's menu, incidentally, shows an unusual variety, including as it does not only the most diverse mammals from the moose to the mouse but also all kinds of birds, fish and even invertebrates like snails. This enormous adaptability with regard to its food, its so-called euryphagy, is closely connected with the above-mentioned wide distribution of the animal both horizontally and vertically. The mountain lion adapts itself to any kind of habitat from the depth of the canyons to snow-covered mountain peaks.

Its main diet is deer and hares. But other mammals occasionally eaten by the mountain lion include such strange prey as the tree porcupine (or urson) and the skunk which one would think were sufficiently protected by their armour of spines in the one case and highly effective stench gland in the other. But there is no such thing as absolute protection in the animal kingdom; even venomous and spine-bristling species have their enemies who have their own peculiar methods of overcoming even such highly specialized defensive equipment.

164

The stomach contents of some mountain lions have been found to contain up to 80 per cent, and even 100 per cent, of tree porcupines. Many of its spines are eaten together with the animal. Clearly these are softened by the digestive juices; in any case they can pass through the intestine, in whole clusters, bundled more or less parallel, without causing damage. But how does the mountain lion manage to kill and eat such a bristling quarry without the barbed spines entering into its paws and mouth in the way this happens to inexperienced hunting dogs in often the most pitiful manner? Admittedly mountain lions have been killed with porcupine spines sticking in their flesh—which undoubtedly was extremely painful. But various observers claim that the mountain lion is able to pull out with its teeth any spines that have entered its skin. A number of questions still await answering, including the one of how the mountain lion manages to kill skunks and at least partially eat them as has been proved by stomach analysis.

Whenever the mountain lion succeeds in killing a large prey, such as a mule-deer or a collared peccary, one of those attractive wild pigs, it obviously cannot consume the whole of it at one go. Whatever remains after its first generous meal is then stored for the future. For this the mountain lion has its own special method; indeed each type of cat has its own. The African leopard, for instance, is in the habit of dragging even antelopes up trees and anchoring them among the branches. In this way the prey is safe both from the ubiquitous hyenas and jackals and from pouncing vultures whose huge wings stop them from venturing among the branches.

The mountain lion's method is quite different: it drags its prey to a suitable spot and there covers it with earth, twigs, branches, stones, dry leaves, moss, etc. This is sometimes done so thoroughly that

absolutely nothing is visible of the buried prey.

The first filling of its stomach will suffice the mountain lion for something like three days. After that the hidden reserves will be approached again and these repeated visits may extend over ten days, according to the temperature and the state of the preservation of the flesh. It can be quite chilly and even cold in the Grand Canyon. Under a snow cover the remains of raw meat may keep for several weeks.

Sometimes the mountain lion may have difficulty in finding a suitable hiding place for its meat store. Instances are known of a slain goat, for instance, being dragged over a third of a mile until a suitable hiding place was found.

Many people believe—on the basis of the experience of zoos—that the mountain lion while roaming free kills a quarry each day. But this is no more the case than it is with the lion or tiger; instead observation of mountain lions in freedom has shown that—like their big African relations—they go hunting only every third or fourth day. In between they digest at leisure, at the quietest possible spot. As for water, the mountain lion is far more independent than the big cats of Africa.

Unlike these, incidentally, the mountain lion is far less often shown in circuses. There are several reasons for this. To begin with, it looks far less impressive in the ring than the African lion which is three times as heavy and moreover adorned with a mane. Only connoisseurs will appreciate the exceptional appearance of mountain lions in a mixed group.

There is yet another reason. I was given a demonstration of it when a lion tamer friend invited me to enter the ring with him: there were three mountain lions in it who were about to be taught the basic elements of drill, i.e. they were to be made to take up their places

on top of blocks and sit erect on their haunches.

This sounds fairly straightforward and with lions or tigers, for instance, represents no problem at all. With these one always knows their mood and their next movement. Their varied expressions, their differentiated gestures and mime, and above all their vocal utterances always reveal to the expert how the animals feel and how far they can be pushed.

Things are totally different and much more difficult with the mountain lion. Here there is no gradual crescendo of grimace or hissing but only an almost chronic laying back of the ears and then an abrupt hiss, or rather a spitting—and the dangerous leap can occur at once. This as a rule aims at the throat, i.e. at the carotids which are only too vulnerable to those terrible claws. My trainer was lucky. A few days after his kindly demonstration I met him with a thick bandage round his neck.

In the wild—and this includes the Grand Canyon—the mountain lion lives together with a smaller and weaker rival, the bobcat (Lynx rufus). Between mountain lion and bobcat there is a similar relationship as between lion and leopard in Africa. This is known as a biological hierarchy, i.e. a hierarchy of species in analogy to the hierarchy of individuals found within a species, which is sometimes described as social hierarchy. This biological hierarchy is encountered with species whose distribution areas overlap or coincide, just as their biotopes, with species, moreover, which are of similar physical organization and hence lead a similar kind of life. All this applies to mountain lion and bobcat; the two species stand to each other in a relationship of biological rivalry, with the much more demanding mountain lion clearly being the superior partner.

Wherever the mountain lion appears the smaller and inferior bobcat has to give way. It is part of a biological hierarchy that the members

of such a system are not in an enemy-quarry relationship—e.g.

mountain lion and tree porcupine or bobcat and squirrel. The inferior partner, as a rule, is not attacked and eaten but must merely yield whenever the superior partner establishes a claim to space or food. Only in exceptional situations is the inferior partner also regarded as prey by the superior, and treated accordingly. Ernest Thompson Seton, whom most readers of the older generation will know as a poet and the author of charming animal stories, at the beginning of the century also published a magnificent eight-volume scientific work on the life of North American wild animals. In it this knowledgeable observer and artist, without knowing anything about our modern concept of biological hierarchy, described this exceedingly typical behavior of the mountain lion which will occasionally attack and eat bobcats when they come upon them helplessly caught in traps. This is an exceedingly typical account of biological hierarchy, of the rivalry of related species. Naturally, the inferior partner of a biological hierarchy also enjoys various advantages over his superior rival: it needs less space, less food and—this is most important—less cover. The bobcat which weighs barely 22 pounds, i.e. about one-tenth of the mountain lion, suceeds in maintaining itself in areas where the mountain lion has long ceased to find adequate conditions of subsistence.

Small wonder therefore that the bobcat has been able to inhabit virtually all the states of the U.S.A. Toward the north its spread has always been limited by the presence of a much more closely related and vicious biological rival, the big Canada lynx *(Lynx canadensis)* to which, however, access to the south, into the Grand Canyon, was absolutely barred.

Descriptions have been published of over a dozen different races of the bobcat whose demands are very much more modest than those of his nearest relation. This exceedingly adaptable wild cat has been able to this day to support itself in appreciable numbers even under the seasonally fluctuating conditions of the Grand Canyon. The bobcat, which will content itself with mice and quails, therefore provokes the farmer's vengeance to a far lesser degree than the mountain lion which harasses their stock.

It is even credibly stated that the bobcat gets on amicable terms with the domestic cats of farmers and even hybridizes with them—a circumstance attested also with regard to other lynxes. Quite certainly it does not eat the cats.

A very similar relationship of biological hierarchy is found also among the wild dogs, i.e. between wolf and coyote. Admittedly nowadays the wild dogs in the Grand Canyon are represented only by coyote and fox—predominantly by the coyote or prairie wolf, a kind of miniature version of the wolf, an exceedingly adaptable animal and capable of living under a great variety of conditions. The wolf proper, which is larger, is more often found in the open plains; steep slopes and narrow gorges are not so much to the liking of this predator, which pursues the game.

Mention must also be made of another, though very much smaller, beast of prey of the marten family—the striped skunk *(Spilogale),* a small weasel-like relation of the skunk proper. Like it, the striped skunk has a much coveted silky fur; but it is also equipped with the same terrible stench weapon. This is a glandular secretion which is squirted backward at enemies with assured aim and produces a frightful effect. It contains a genuine poison gas, butyl mercaptan; this makes the eyes smart and immediately puts any effective attacker to flight. Even humans can faint from it; houses in which a discharge has taken place remain uninhabitable for weeks or months; stretches of country can remain contaminated if a skunk has been run over by an automobile.

When discharging their malodorous poison these otherwise so charming little animals tip their tail upwards and sometimes perform a handstand. The hairs around the gland orifice are turned outward to ensure that the little beast itself remains entirely clean. These animals can only be kept on farms and in zoos if their frightful glands have previously been surgically removed—of course with the necessary precautions.

Such doctored skunks make most charming and loving pets and occasionally earn their keep by exterminating mice and rats and other vermin. They are particularly fond of eating all kinds of insects such as beetles and grasshoppers which in liberty form their main diet. Now and again a squirrel may fall victim to a skillful climber.

Its four or five young, which are identifiable even at that stage by the typical black-and-white patterning of their adult fur, are born as a rule in a specially dug hollow among roots or under rocks. Now and again the hole of ground squirrels may be taken over, enlarged and used as a home.

Another small predator that must not be left out even from a brief survey is the cacomistle *(Bassariscus astutus)*—especially as this attractive and very curious representative of the Procyonidae is very rarely seen in European zoos. The cacomistle is related to the better-known racoon, coati and kinkajou. In America this animal, roughly the size of a marten, bears a variety of names which all basically reflect the same embarrassment—uncertainty where to place this strange creature among the small mammals. The most common of these names are cacomistle or cacomixl; the latter has a Mexican ring about it and suggests—quite correctly—that this attractive little animal is found not only in the Southwest of the U.S.A. but also in Mexico and in Central America beyond.

Names like racoon-fox, coon-cat, cat-squirrel, civet-fox, etc., all suggest that this ringed-tailed procyonid shows external similarities with racoon, cat, squirrel, fox, etc. One simply must have seen the animal to form a proper idea of it. But just that is by no means easy. Even Thompson Seton expressed surprise in his monumental work about the wild animals of North America that many farmers living right in the middle of the distribution area of the cacomistle, or even in areas where it is particularly common, have never seen one. This is due, of course, to the fact that it is a predominantly nocturnal animal.

Among the most striking wild animals of the Grand Canyon—after the beasts of prey—are a number of ungulates. Pronghorn and Dickson's horned sheep are unlikely ever to venture down into the depths of the canyon from the neighbouring areas. The mule-deer, on the other hand, is relatively common, as is also its close relation the white-tailed deer, especially its graceful Arizona race. These representatives of the tailed deer are exceedingly skillful climbers in the vertically dissected surroundings, comparable in a sense to the European chamois which is not daunted either by the steepest rock-faces or the deepest yawning precipices.

Unfortunately it is not possible to give anything like a complete picture here of the great variety and fascination of the fauna of the Grand Canyon. We can only pick out a few representatives, especially those reproduced in the photographs. Among the rodents the tree porcupine, the urson *(Erethizon dorsatum)*, undoubtedly occupies such a prominent position that we have to devote some attention to it. We have already come across this rodent as a favourite prey of the mountain lion in spite of its armor of roughly 30,000 spines.

As its name suggests we shall encounter it only in the tree-grown zones. It is only there, and more especially in coniferous forests, that these exceedingly skillful climbers find their food which includes fresh tree bark, twigs and young shoots—sufficient reason to label the animal a forest pest. Added to this are its slow movements, its predominantly nocturnal mode of life and, last not least, its bristly pelt. All these are characteristics which humans as a rule regard as unattractive.

Anyone, however, who takes the trouble to look more closely at these seemingly unapproachable spiky creatures, especially anyone observing young animals in captivity, without prejudice or indeed lovingly, will soon agree that these maligned pests are in fact undeniably charming creatures.

One of the more prominent champions of the urson is Albert R. Shadle of the University of Buffalo. He has immersed himself sympathetically in the character of these porcupines, he has observed them as domestic pets at close quarters at all times of the day and night, he has brought up their young and has even repreatedly been a witness to mating and birth—processes about which, in view of the animal's spines, somewhat fantastic ideas used to exist even among zoologists. In this understanding atmosphere there was even opportunity for a close study of all kinds of games and dance-like behavior patterns—manifestations with which these apparently dull creatures had never been credited before. It is significant that Shadle described these unexpected findings in the Journal of Comparative Psychology (Volume 37). Making contact with an animal reputed to be strange is, after all, a matter of so-called comparative psychology which embraces animals and humans.

In the course of prolonged intimate contact with these bristly rodents it was clearly inevitable that Professor Shadle should also make the acquaintance of the much-feared barbed spines—a circumstance which in a sense rounded off his picture of the urson.

It had always been asserted that any *Erethizon* spine which had once entered into the flesh of a victim would, because of its barbed structure and the automatic muscle movements, inevitably move further and deeper. Shadle's involuntary experiment on himself did not refute this thesis—on the contrary.

On the occasion of the birth of an urson—an exciting zoological event in itself—the scholar was naturally anxious to measure and weigh the new-born animal because such data are exceedingly rarely obtained. While he was doing this a spine of the young animal, only just over half an inch long, penetrated into his right forearm. At first he did not even notice it—but seven hours later the foreign body signalled its presence most unpleasantly. During the attempt to pull the barbed spine out of the wound it broke twice. Urgent work made Shadle temporarily forget this slight incident— the more so as he attached no particular importance to it. After all, this was the delicate spine of a new-born urson; it was not causing any acute pain and, moreover, was relatively sterile.

After 42 hours, however, the point of the spine once more called attention to itself as it was emerging from the skin. Only now was it possible to withdraw it and Shadle found that it had travelled about 42 millimetres under the skin—i.e. roughly a millimetre per hour. It is obvious that the large spines of fully grown animals, which would undoubtedly be infected, could, if they got deep into the flesh, cause painful and slow-healing wounds, and, under certain circumstances, even the death of a victim affected by more than one.

It would be quite wrong, even in the most cursory survey of the fauna of the Grand Canyon, to omit the great variety of birds from the hummingbird to the eagle. The eagle, known in America as the golden eagle, is indeed the most powerful of the local birds, and moreover revered as a national symbol—but in popularity it is surpassed by the roadrunner, a bird barely the size of a crow, with a curved beak, by no means pretty and scarcely capable of flight. Its scientific name is *Geococcyx californianus.*

This widespread bird—which is in fact a cuckoo living on the ground— is, of course, also found in the Grand Canyon. Its enormous popularity is no doubt largely due to the fact that it is a passionate exterminator of snakes. It will bravely attack even the most venomous rattlesnakes and, thanks to its incredible swiftness, will hack out its brain in battle at the right fraction of a second. Even though this dangerous prey can never be entirely accommodated in its stomach the bird immediately gets down to consuming its vanquished poisonous enemy.

This it does by unconcernedly starting with the head and forcing as much of the snake's body down as it can manage for the moment. As the swallowed part is digested and passed on into the intestine the remaining part gradually flows; that is why roadrunners are quite frequently found with a portion of a snake still hanging out of their beak.

The bird is known as a runner because it mostly declines to use its wings but instead races along the ground at great speed. On open ground without obstacles, admittedly, a fast human runner can still outrace it. Its running speed has been estimated at 15 miles per hour and it is claimed that, although it can fly, it will get up to a branch about 6 feet above ground not by flying but by leaping with wings folded back.

The astonishing speed developed by the roadrunner has, not surprisingly perhaps, lent wings to the fantasy of human observers, and not only in respect of its speed of locomotion but also of a startling rapidity of braking. This is an instance of typical humanization, i.e. the transference of human and technological behavior patterns to biological events. This is always a mistake, as shown by

174  other examples from wildlife. One person will suggest it to another,

one writer will copy it from another: surely a bird sweeping over the ground at such speed must also possess a highly effective brake. And so we find—each book referring to another—the persistent information that in order to stop its rapid run the roadrunner elevates its tail, rather like a short-landing-path aircraft using a parachute brake. This view is totally wrong. The tail, or rather the tail feathers, have in fact no braking function. True, they are raised when halting the run, but that is done by many other birds, including the blackbird. Not a single bird uses its tail feathers for deceleration on the ground. After all, there would have to be specialized muscles present and nothing is known in bird anatomy about such muscles.

All the cuckoos—and there are over 200 species—possess long tail feathers: not only the roadrunner but also the tropical cuckoos which move by slipping through dense foliage. This characteristic is therefore shared by the roadrunner, and the elevation of its tail when halting its run is something it has in common with many other birds. Why it does so we do not know, any more than we understand the "meaning" of the tail wagging of wagtails and many other species.

It is not surprising that such a well-loved and popular bird as the snake-killing roadrunner is made the subject of numerous legends which are occasionally confused with actual observations. We will mention just one such legend: this refers to the killing of snakes, an ability which naturally excites human fantasy to a particular degree.

Thus it is claimed that the roadrunner carefully builds a prickly circle of about 3 feet diameter around a sleeping rattlesnake. For material it uses pieces of cacti which it collects in the neighborhood until the wall is about 4 inches high. Then the bird drops a particularly prickly piece directly on to the snake so that it starts and wildly thrashes about. This causes more and more cactus spines to enter under its scales, wounding it so severely that the bird can then kill it without much effort. But how can it then eat a snake full of spines? This fairy-tale is reminiscent of that of the scorpion being surrounded with a circle of fire. The poisonous arthropod first tries to escape from the flames but when it discovers this to be impossible it commits suicide by stabbing itself with its own venomous tail sting. Needless to say there is no truth whatever in this equally persistent legend.

The largest and most impressive bird encountered in the Grand Canyon—though only occasionally—is the golden eagle. The "gold" refers to a yellowish coloring of the head which is found in older birds.

Obviously this powerful bird of prey has long disappeared from Eastern America; only in the West does it still, in certain regions, find the living conditions it needs—undisturbed landscapes of rock and woodland where its favorite prey is present in sufficient quantities. This includes fawns, hares, coyotes, ground squirrels, etc., as well as birds up to the size of turkeys.

Among nocturnal birds of prey the biggest is the great horned owl (Bubo virginianus). Its "horns", however, are merely fine feathers projecting in two tufts from both sides of its head.

The mourning dove (Zenaidura macroura) is hunted by the major diurnal and nocturnal birds of prey. Its name is another case of humanization: man reads a melancholy mourning note into its call which, of course, no more reflects a melancholy disposition than that of Turtur risorius, the Barbary dove, known in some languages as the "laughing dove", reflects hilarity.

The macroura part of the name means "large-tailed". This characteristic, together with some others, leads to a certain resemblance

176 with its now extinct relation the passenger pigeon (Ectopistes

*migratoria)*. This has been totally extinct since 1914 but used to be present in North America in unimaginable numbers—their mass flights darkened the sky. Mighty trees snapped under the weight of swarms of tens of thousands settling on them. Then a galloping extermination set in, comparable to that of the American buffalo. In 1900 a mere 50 or so passenger pigeons were left of what used to be countless millions. The last specimen, known as Martha, died on September 1, 1914, at 5.00 p.m. in Cincinnati Zoo.

Only then were the implications of this senseless and shameful deed realized. A few idealists did not give up all hope and offered a prize of 5,000 dollars to whoever could prove the existence of a breeding pair of passenger pigeons. Numerous reports were, of course, received but in all instances they proved to be cases of confusion with the still widespread mourning dove, which—as we have said—also inhabits the Grand Canyon.

A territory which offers so many different and varied habitats as the Grand Canyon naturally also contains a great number of interesting reptiles—i.e. tortoises, lizards and snakes. Crocodiles are totally absent from this arid territory with its turbulent and mostly cold river. They prefer warm and calm waters. From among the wealth of other reptiles all we can do here is pick out the most prominent which are also illustrated in this book—the sidewinder among the snakes and the so-called Gila monster among the lizards.

Let us deal with the Gila monster first. This is a lizard of no more than about 20 inches long, with the scientific name *Heloderma suspectum.* This lizard, which is perfectly adapted to its arid hot habitat and which, because of its bead-like scales, is also known as the beaded lizard, is not just "suspect" but is quite clearly one of the dangerous venomous lizards. There are roughly 3,000 different species of lizard and only two of these, fortunately, are venomous—

the Gila monster and its close relation *Heloderma horridum* which is confined to Mexico. A third species which had been suspected of being venomous—it occurs in Borneo—proved to be harmless.

The Gila monster has its much-feared poison fangs not in the upper jaw—as in all venomous snakes—but in its lower jaw. The bite of this Arizona lizard can have very dangerous, and in rare cases even lethal, effects. Naturally this venomous creature does not lurk behind every cactus or under every stone in order to pounce on the first human. It feeds almost exclusively on the eggs of ground-breeding birds. It becomes dangerous only when one tries to pick it up, either in order to capture it or to carry it to a more favorable spot for photography. Zoo attendants are in the habit of picking up this dangerous creature as if it were a harmless tortoise. Many even begin to regard the danger of this lizard as a superstition merely because nothing has been heard of venomous bites for a number of years. This leads to carelessness.

Sure enough, every ten years or so some frightening case of a bite is reported and this may take weeks or even months to heal. The odd thing about the behavior of the Gila monster is that in captivity it acts like a slow-motion creature, i.e. it drags itself along quite slowly—if it moves at all. It will slurp up its food—egg yolk with mince meat—with a provoking slowness, and often only when its mouth has been pushed into the bowl. Then suddenly, quite abruptly, this extreme slowness or lethargy flicks over into lightning-like movements, for instance if a *Heloderma* is exposed to direct sunlight for the purpose of photography. Then the lizard can throw itself about unpredictably, like an angry bulldog, and snap with lightning speed. If it has bitten a finger it will lock its jaws like 178 a pair of pliers and without suitable tools the finger cannot be released again. Meanwhile an alarming amount of poison can flow into the wound.

The eerie thing about such bites is not so much the painful local effect but the central disturbances which are produced—such as failure of memory and association of ideas, inability to perform intended movements or actions, etc. The toxic effect of a bite can be made worse by all kinds of infections such as gas gangrene and tetanus. There is no other rule than "hands off Gila monsters". C.M. Bogert and R.M. del Campo in their magnificent monograph on the *Heloderma* ("The Gila Monster and its Allies" in: Bull. Am. Mus. Nat. Hist. 109, Article 1, New York 1956) have described no fewer than 34 cases of bites. It is significant that not a single of them occurred at the Grand Canyon; most of them were caused by careless handling of the dangerous reptile in laboratories and zoos.

Much the same applies to the second reptile to be discussed here—the so-called sidewinder *(Crotalus cerastes)*. This snake, also known as the horned rattlesnake, is merely one of 14 rattlesnakes occurring in Arizona alone, but—as its name suggests—noteworthy not because of its considerable venomousness but because of its strange way of locomotion.

Snakes have several different methods of locomotion. The sidewinder belongs to the rare species which, when crawling in the sand, leave not a continuous but a broken track. On the entire globe there are only two other species moving in this manner—one in the desert areas of Northern Africa and the other in the deserts of South-West Africa. This is clearly a good example of convergence—i.e. independent adaptation to a certain habitat, in this case dry hot sand—by unrelated species.

This "sidewinding", roughly speaking, is performed by the snake using one coil of its body behind its head and another before its tail in the manner of feet, alternately lifting them and putting them down. This produces the entirely unusual track which used to puzzle observers a great deal. It was thought at one time that these were the tracks of crippled snakes; nowadays this strange method of locomotion has been studied in great detail on the basis of film analysis.

The term horned rattlesnake merely reflects the fact that this venomous snake carries a group of erect soft scales on both sides of his head. These skin formations, of course, are entirely harmless. At one time there was a superstition that the snake stung its victims with these "horns"; its tongue, too, was regarded as a dangerous organ. Needless to say, all venomous snakes bite or sting with their highly specialized fangs. In the case of the rattlesnake and its relations, i.e. all pit vipers and other vipers, these are cannular curved hollow needles which are thrust forward from the snake's oral cavity and squirt the venom into the wound under pressure.

The Gila monster and the sidewinder are not the only venomous animals in the Grand Canyon; there are quite a few venomous invertebrates, especially among the insects, spiders, centipedes and other arthropods. After all, venom or poison in the biological sense is not a homogeneous dangerous substance possessed by one group of animals or another. Animal poisons instead must be understood as exceedingly effective digestive juices whose primary purpose is digestion; defense, as a rule, is only a secondary purpose in the absence of other weapons.

Venom therefore represents a chemical weapon for the defeat of an animal's prey or for its defence against superior enemies when no other weapons—especially mechanical weapons such as teeth, claws, horns, antlers, hooves, etc.,—are available. Provision is made throughout the animal kingdom that weapons are never totally

absent but equally that there should be no excessive accumulation of weapons. They are, in a manner of speaking, fairly distributed. Each species is endowed with sufficiently effective weapons to give it a good chance of preservation. These are mechanical, psychological or even electrical weapons (as with certain fishes), but they can also be chemical weapons of the kind used by venomous animals. The urson enjoys relatively effective mechanical protection in its many thousands of spines, just as the mountain lion is well armed with his teeth and claws; the Gila monster and sidewinder, on the other hand, rely extensively on their chemical weapons, i.e. their venom. It should be repeated, however, that there is no such thing as absolute protection anywhere in the animal kingdom: even the urson can fall victim to the mountain lion, and the rattlesnake to the roadrunner.

Among venomous centipedes, scorpions and spiders mention should briefly be made of the tarantula. In the Grand Canyon and its neighborhood one occasionally sees very large furry spiders scurrying over the ground; these are two or three inches long. They resemble the South American bird spiders but do not catch birds any more than do the South American species; instead they feed chiefly on grasshoppers and other insects which they catch without a web. Even small lizards and geckos are occasionally seized by them and sucked dry.

It is as a rule very difficult to assign these large spiders to any species. They are, in a manner of speaking, the problem children of museums where many thousands of specimens are being kept and are still awaiting exact study. There is a shortage of specialized zoologists and hence also a lack of precise information about these creatures. I therefore regard it as somewhat reckless to maintain that the large spiders of the Grand Canyon are entirely harmless and may be safely picked up. I would be inclined to advise, as a matter of general principle, to leave the spiders and all other venomous animals alone and not to provoke them needlessly.

This concludes our brief survey of the fauna of the Grand Canyon. Mention should be made in conclusion of the countless magnificent butterflies and birds, of the colorful lizards and attractively patterned small mammals which give pleasure to the visitor of this unique giant gorge. But he must also bear in mind the possibility of encounters with the bristling urson, the bobcat or even the mountain lion. As I said at the beginning of this chapter, it was possible only to pick out a very few of the large number of canyon inhabitants. Like the magnificent colors of the Grand Canyon so the aspects of its fauna also change according to the time of day and the season: each of these is fascinating in its own way and full of surprises.

Heini Hediger

Brief captions

78  Small forest lake on the North Rim (Kaibab Forest)
79  Coyote at the Grand Canyon
80  Mule-deer in Kaibab Forest
81  Yellow-haired urson
82  Mule-deer on the edge of Kaibab Forest
83  Mule-deer
84  Close-up of a mule-deer
85  Golden eagle
86  Young mountain lion padding along lethargically
87  Bobcat
88  Half-grown mountain lions
89  Young mountain lion adopting defensive posture
90  Mule-deer in the forest shade
91  Close-up of golden eagle
92  Mountain lion in typical canyon landscape
93  Fully grown mountain lion
94  Young mountain lion still showing youthful
     spotted fur
95  Spotted skunk
96  Cacomistle
97  Mourning dove, hatching on *Opuntia fulgida*
98  Bobcat
99  Young mountain lions
100  Mountain lion lazily stretching in the spring sun
101–117  Roadrunner
118  Young bobcat
119  Mountain lion in defensive attitude
120  Gray fox
121  Sidewinder
122  Track of a sidewinder
123  Gila monster
124  Tarantula spider
125  Coyote near the precipice
126  Gray foxes
127  Coyote in typical canyon landscape
128  Great horned owl

86

87

95

96

102

103

104

105

106

107

108

109

110

111

112

113

114

115

116

117

119

120

123

124

# A Year at the Grand Canyon

My husband and I lived at the Grand Canyon for a full year filming a 35 mm Cinemascope motion picture, "The Grand Canyon", a pictorial representation of Ferde Grofe's famous musical composition, "The Grand Canyon Suite". It was a great adventure to use music as the script for the first time, to do everything in reverse and to make the pictures fit to music already composed. And it was a rather overwhelming experience to live with the Grand Canyon for an entire year, struggling constantly with the problems of filming in snow and ice, with the wind raging and ripping, or the sun beating down on us until we were dripping wet.

Day after day, week after week, month after month we went out before sunrise, put up our camera and waited for one of nature's changing moods—for clouds that boil like lava, a mantle of winter snow, the lazing flight of an eagle, another scene which would fit into our motion picture. Why had we done it? And how had the Grand Canyon come to loom so large in our lives?

When the idea was born to make a pictorial representation of Ferde Grofe's, "The Grand Canyon Suite", neither Ernst nor I had seen the great abyss. We liked the music with its five movements which are self-descriptive: *Sunrise, Painted Desert, Sunset, Cloudburst* and *On the Trail.* It was decided that no traces of human beings should be included, that the wildlife and the Canyon itself should tell the story.

Ernst had taught me a little about the art of motion picture making, at least enough so that I could work as a camera assistant and script girl. Therefore, I was able to take part in the wonderful adventure. I had never been the outdoor type and knew next to nothing of nature. I even had a great fear of most animals—so quite a few surprises were in store. It was fortunate that Ernst was well schooled in psychology. He had a gentle way of dealing with me from the very beginning, of getting me familiar with the animals, reptiles and insects, of introducing me step by step to darkness, to wind and rain, to violent thunderstorms and snowstorms.

He displayed a tremendous confidence in me—then left me on my own. Under such circumstances, although often terrified, how could I show my fear? I was too proud. I hid my fear for a long time but eventually I became master of it. At last, I could stand two feet away from a poisonous sidewinder rattlesnake without flinching, thinking only of the picture, or I could remain in an electrical thunderstorm and be fascinated by the play of lightning against the metal- of our tripod. I was able to "shoot the rapids" down the Colorado River, to be thrilled by the adventure of a rapid so swift that we almost lost our rubber pontoon boats. To have been thrown into a swirling rapid would have been a disaster for me as I could not swim. But all of this was much later...

We arrived at the South Rim of the Grand Canyon one late afternoon in early March. We were at once overwhelmed by this gigantic gorge which is 4 to 18 miles wide, 217 miles long and is cut by the mighty Colorado River which empties in the Gulf of California in Mexico. Rising from the Canyon's depths are rims and mountains towering up toward the sky. It is a magnificent spectacle. There are thousands of rock temples and buttes, ever-changing in color and mood.

We stood transfixed until the sun set and the reds deepened to dim purples and the yellows and greens changed to magical blues. Then night fell and it was terribly mysterious. The outlines of the great abyss were soon visible in silver light. The stars there seemed to be brighter than stars anywhere else and sometimes they appeared to float up from the sky.

We rented a room at the El Tovar Hotel which is situated on the very brink of this chasm. It is a long, low, rambling structure made

of native pine logs. We unpacked our clothes, camera equipment and record player. We had brought along only one recording, "The Grand Canyon Suite", which was actually to be used as the script for our movie. The next morning we were up before dawn to observe our first sunrise over the Canyon. We drove twenty-five miles to the Desert View Point where the historical Indian watchtower is located and from which one has a superb view. At first it was eerie and somewhat frightening. The black of night still embraced the Canyon and we were utterly alone. We could hear the constant roar of the Colorado River. Languidly, and with an ethereal quality, the break of day began. The light softened the darkness as dawn moved over the Grand Canyon.

It was quite an emotional experience, this first sunrise over the Canyon, with everything so soft and pink and mystical. The outlines of the great abyss became recognizable. Suddenly, we could distinguish the Colorado River far down below. Finally, there was life and radiance. It was then that I saw something moving at the edge of the Canyon. Ernst told me not to be alarmed and to stand perfectly still. He is convinced that most animals attack only in self defense. "It's only a harmless gopher snake that we have disturbed", he laughed. "Later on you will be holding it in your hands." He taught me to display no fear if I wanted to be the master of an animal. Ernst grew up with horses and has a deep love for all animals. "An animal sees immediately in your eyes and actions whether or not you are afraid", he said.

Days passed, idyllic weeks; we had become intimate friends with the Canyon. We observed it from a thousand different aspects, from dawn to dusk until there was not a single ray of light left to distinguish its form, trying to understand its moods, to fathom its secrets—the mysteries in which it enveloped itself. "We could probably unravel some of the secrets of life itself if only we could understand what it is trying to tell us", Ernst said. One thing we knew for sure—it dwarfed man and made him inconsequential in comparison.

We were always on the spot ready to film but sometimes we had to wait long hours or even days for a single picture. Therefore, we had plenty of time to study nature, the plants and vegetation. We watched the day to day growth of the flowers and shrubs, the miraculous first opening of a blossom, swarms of dragonflies appearing suddenly from out of nowhere, a hummingbird building a beautiful nest.

Actually, we became ardent birdwatchers. Ornithologists estimate that there are about 180 species of birds in the Grand Canyon National Park and I think that we saw most of them at one time or another. I was ever intrigued by the great horned owl with tufts of feathers protruding above his enormous eyes. It was a curious fact to me that I could discern no sound whatsoever when he was in flight. Although covered with feathers, when he flew there was no rustling of wings. I supposed that this was another of nature's ingenious ways of protecting him. And, I regarded with wonder and delight the mourning dove who was clever enough to build her nest high up in a cholla cactus so that her young could grow and learn the facts of bird life in relative safety.

But, of course, the one that I admired the most was the golden eagle, the king of birds, which is large and powerful and now somewhat rare to behold. The one we filmed was a lordly creature with an approximate five-foot wing span. Once he soared into the air until he was barely distinguishable, then folded his wings and dived down to earth. It appeared as if he would crash, but at the very last moment he unfolded his wings and with great momentum

soared again to an enormous height over the majestic temples and buttes. He seemed to be demonstrating to all of his feathered cousins in the vicinity that, although indeed rare, he was still king of birds.

To know the Canyon one must walk through it, so we explored the inner depths by taking the trails which lead down to the Colorado River. First, we made the trip by muleback along the Bright Angel Trail. Down, down, down winds the trail, each turn opening up new, magnificent vistas. Approximately half way down we stopped at the Indian Gardens, after which the trail stretches out upon the Tonto Plateau and then heads downward through the Granite Gorge to the banks of the Colorado River. Next, we took the Kaibab Trail from the North Rim, which descends into the Canyon through aspen, fir, pine and oak brush to the Redwall limestone section. The trail enters Bright Angel Canyon at the mouth of the Manzanita Creek. In this section of the Grand Canyon area we saw a spectacular waterfall, gushing forth beneath the Redwall limestone, cascading down to the gorge forty feet below.

We also explored the surrounding areas of the Grand Canyon, a vast region covering approximately four thousand square miles. Mexico borders the Canyon to the South, to the North lies Utah and the famous city of Las Vegas, to the East is New Mexico and to the West, the Death Valley of California. We were fascinated by the Painted Desert and the Petrified Forest. The Painted Desert extends for about 300 miles along the North side of the Little Colorado River. First seen by the Spaniards in the 1500's—they named it Desierto Pintado—it is a colorful, eroded badlands of Bentonitic beds (volcanic ash) stained with shades of red, orange, yellow, blue, purple and brown. The most important coloring agent is simple iron rust. Arid or semi-arid with only a sparse vegetation cover, these soft beds are subject to rapid erosion during Arizona's season of torrential rains. Here the dry dust drifts with the wind, and the occasional violent rainstorms pelt the crumbling shales and limestone, each drop leaving its imprint on the spongy, bentonitic clay.

The Painted Desert formed a barrier behind which the early Hopi Indians withdrew to establish their famed mesa-top villages, including Oraibi which has been continuously occupied since about 350 years before the discovery of America. These people still live in their several mesa-top villages, their reservation surrounded by that of the Navajo, their former enemies, who now lead a peaceful, semi-nomadic life. Nearby, paleontologists have collected fossil remains, dating back to the beginning of the rise of the dinosaurs. It must be quite a surprise to come upon the track of a great three-toed monster which was imprinted there some two hundred million years ago.—The Painted Desert, with its rolling mounds of painted sand, is a fine example of erosion. According to a geologist, it is constantly being recreated in its own destruction. We found it beautiful, mysterious and lonely. There is a stillness—a profound silence.

The Petrified Forest with its spectacular display of "stone trees" is unique in vivid and varied colors. Giant logs of agate lie on the ground. These trees lived approximately one hundred and sixty million years ago and the principal tree resembled the native pine of America. Here can be seen an estimated million tons of sparkling jewels, including agate, amethyst, carnelian and jasper. It is an interesting fact that Queen Isabella of Spain's Conquistadors, in their search for the fabled Seven Cities of Cibola, saw and named the Painted Desert, but failed to travel a little farther west to discover this magnificent treasure. It is not until some three hundred years later in the 1850's that we find the first written record

concerning the Petrified Forest.

A ranger told us that quite a number of people visiting the area for the first time are very much surprised to find the forest lying down. The death of the trees, their burial and transformation into dazzling stone is a complicated story. Although many of the trees died of natural processes and decayed on the ground, others fell into streams and came to rest in bays or sand bars where rapid burial by mud and sand prevented their decay. The sediments in which the logs were buried contained a large amount of volcanic ash, rich in silica. This silica was picked up by ground water, carried into the wood, and deposited in the cell tissue. The mineral filled the wood solidly, forming the petrified log. The color patterns were caused by oxides of iron and manganese, the predominant type known as agate. The cavities in the logs are often filled or lined with quartz crystal. Some logs show scars of ancient fires.

There are six separate "forests" within the Petrified Forest National Monument where one finds the greatest concentration of petrified logs. They are called the First, Second, Third, Black, Rainbow, and Blue Forests. Color and form are paramount—red, yellow, brown, blue, green, pink, purple—a kaleidoscope of colors making up a fantastic desert panorama. Agate Bridge, with 111 feet of exposed log, is perhaps the most famous petrified log in the world. The Spanish Conquistadors would surely have been enchanted by this dazzling foot crossing of solid semi-precious stone.

Here and there are beds of shale containing perfectly preserved fossil leaves of plants of a remote age. Many Indian ruins and petroglyphs are found, evidence of Indians who lived in this area long before America was discovered. No animal showed itself to us during the daytime in the Forest but a ranger assured us that it is quite another story at night. Creatures such as bobcats, badger, rabbits, coyote, porcupine, skunk, fox and ground squirrels all dwell in this area. Although there is less than 10 inches of moisture a year, nearby grow the yuccas with their imposing blossoms, the Mariposa lily and cacti of many varieties.

From time to time we encountered Indians from the Hopi or Navajo tribes and we felt a deep sympathy toward them. With few exceptions they were extremely passive. They seemed to have no ambition—no hope for the future. It was hard to imagine that these were the descendants of the fighting red men, the American aborigines. However, we became friends with Navajo shepherds of a somewhat more energetic type. These men had handsome classical faces, wore brilliant colors and rode white horses as they led their sheep over the barren grounds in search of pasturage. The sheep, incidentally, usually belong to the women as most Navajo Indians live under the matriarchal system. However, the shepherds assured us that the horses and cattle are traditionally owned by the men.

Once we chanced upon some Indians burning a hogan, the hut in which they live. A woman had died inside and, according to their belief, it was necessary to burn everything to keep the evil spirits from entering the bodies of other members of the family. A forlorn looking man with three little children and an old grandmother walked away with no possessions except the clothes which they wore.

Most Navajo women wear brilliantly colored silk skirts, velvet blouses and silver jewelry. It is beautifully carved and often set with turquoise stones. It is handed down from generation to generation and they make quite another quality of jewelry for sale in the shops. The squash blossom necklace is a popular one as its meaning is connected with fertility. The women adorn themselves even though they may be weaving rugs or grinding corn. They have a fascinating hair-do. It is similar to a pony tail and is tied in a white cloth. It is

worn in this manner as a continual prayer for rain.

Possession of jewelry, incidentally, has a far deeper significance than just for purposes of adornment. It often reflects the standard of taste and wealth of the tribe. When necessary, it is pawned at the nearest trading post for food and clothing. The jewelry is usually retrieved with wool from the lambs or a woven rug. The Navajo likes smooth, polished silver set with a few large stones. Basically, the Navajos are nature worshipers and their religion is closely inter-woven with the events in their daily lives. Rituals are held for almost everything imaginable—to bring rain, cure disease, insure good crops or for protection when making a journey. The famed sand paintings created by this tribe are also religious expressions. They are made under the supervision of a medicine man. Before sun-down the lovely sand paintings (often depicting mythical beings or sacred mountains) must be destroyed.

The Navajo Reservation is spectacular to behold and covers a vast region of some sixteen million acres. However, most of the soil is wasteland and water is often inaccessible. We traveled extensively on the Reservation, sometimes covering vast areas without seeing a single sprig of green grass. Although most of his soil is eroded beyond use, the Navajo Indian gives thanks and relates in myth and chant the creation of his land by the gods. He lives close to nature and in spite of poverty, famine and disease, I am certain that he would never even consider denuding a forest or polluting a stream.

The Death Valley is a desolate area but it has a stark enchantment and one is ever reminded of the early immigrants dying of thirst as they faced the blazing Death Valley sun. As they creaked along in their wagons, Indians were often lurking to make an attack. The wind blasts its way through mesquite and far across the Valley of Death, spiralling sand spins toplike across the desert. It whirls closer and the sand cascades down a slope. A cloud of sand appeared and afterwards we were surprised to find that Gypsy, our station wagon, no longer had any paint.

Certainly, my most important rememberance about the Death Valley is the heat. It was almost unbearable even in spring. In summer it is not at all unusual to reach 118 degrees Fahrenheit. The record for an official reading was 134.6 attained on July 10, 1913. In the broiling sun we were dripping wet with perspiration so we drank frequently from our canteens. But the water in no way satisfied our thirst. Our throats were dry and parched. We had a constant almost uncontrollable desire for liquid and we began to understand the irrationality and hallucinations of desperately thirsty men. We were surprised at the fascinating array of plant and animal life found in the Valley of Death. The land supports more than 230 species of birds, 17 lizards, 19 snakes and numerous spiders and insects. Plant life is also abundant. Most majestic of Death Valley's animals is the desert bighorn sheep. It is not unusual to find rams weighing 150 pounds or more with thick horns of 25–30 inches long.

In April we made a boat trip down the Colorado River. This is an adventure which has been enjoyed by only a few hundred people in the entire world. It is a never-to-be-forgotten experience, and provides an extraordinary opportunity to view the Grand Canyon. Much of the way lies between great cliffs, towering as high as half a mile above the river, and in places where the walls break back, magnificent vistas are afforded. The rapids are numerous and varied. Some of them are rough—many of them are thrillers—and at least one of them, Lava Falls, is treacherous.

We made the trip with Georgie White, often called "The Woman of the River", for she is the only woman ever to have piloted these dangerous runs. Our reason for choosing Georgie was that her river craft, neoprene barges, provided a safer and steadier base for our movie camera. Three of these rubber rafts were lashed together side by side with nylon rope, making a deck approximately 21 × 28 feet. There are 235 miles of river between Lees Ferry, Arizona, where the adventure began, and our destination, Lake Mead, California. The journey required eighteen days which are etched forever in my memory.

I had never planned to make this trip in tricky waters even though it is considered to be the ultimate in adventure journeys. Not even being able to swim, I thought it was rather ridiculous to go down a wild river on a rubber barge. I had not the slightest desire to thrill to rapids beyond comparison, to view breathtaking sheer canyon walls. I pleaded with Ernst to make the trip alone and to leave me on a beautiful beach where I could spend the days pouring the sand through my toes. However, as he had chartered the boat at a rather high cost, he encouraged me to go along and to participate in the "adventure of a lifetime". Although I was dead set against the whole idea, one day I found myself standing beside him in an army surplus store as he purchased the following items: a light air mattress, sleeping bag, plastic rainsuit, nylon jacket, shorts, blue jeans and tennis shoes. "We'll buy everything for you, too, just in case..." he teased.

At Lees Ferry the water was so placid and listless that I needed no further coaxing to join the party. I felt quite ashamed that I had ever been afraid. To Ernst's delight I got caught up in the excitement of making the journey and shoved off with the others without uttering a word of protest. Our luggage, enclosed in rubberized-waterproof duffle bags, was tied securely to the ropes on top of the barge. The center raft was equipped with an 18 horsepower outboard motor to facilitate landing and maneuvering in the current, as the barge was 227 too unwieldy for oars to be effective.

The sun was shining and the weather was mild. The landscape was open and friendly. With the help of the motor we were traveling at a speed of about ten miles an hour. We were surrounded by the beautiful red rocks of the Marble Canyon area and the muddy Colorado River stretched out in front of us for as far as the eye could follow.

The first rapids (Badger Creek, Soap Creek, House Rock and Twenty-Nine Mile Rapid) offered only a thrilling introduction to the sport of rough water boating. However, a few days later I had many occasions to regret not having stayed at home on the beach. But, although I was indeed frightened, as there was no way of escape at that stage, I decided to face the situation as calmly as possible. There are very few places in the 235 miles of river where it is possible to climb out to the rim. For the most part, the river itself must be relied upon as means of escape.

At night we pulled ashore, anchored the boat and scrambled up a steep rock to make camp. Dan Davis, park ranger and veteran riverman, gave us much information about the lower section of the Canyon. He also had many dramatic and adventurous tales to tell for he was responsible for rescuing people lost or stranded on the river. Once he had to rescue a man who tried to shoot the rapids in a barrel. And he explained that a few individuals are willing to risk their lives to reach a remote section of the Canyon in search of loot. The loot they are after, largely jewelry, is part of the remaining débris from a tragic airplane crash of 1956 when a DC-7 and a Super Constellation collided in mid-air over the Grand Canyon killing 128 people.

While on the river I spent most of my time holding on to the nylon ropes, bailing out water, and speculating as to what might wait

beyond. I tried desperately to figure out what thoughts Ernst might be having. However, there was an air of nonchalance about him, and as far as I could tell, he seemed to be completely indifferent to the danger ahead.

The Canyon walls grew narrow, the cliffs rose ever higher and the water became swifter. The air was filled with a deafening roar. Ernst yelled at me to "hold on" and I knew that we were in for some rough boating ahead. I dug my fingers deeper into the ropes to secure a better hold. I wondered what my heart rate was. I had not much time to think about what was going to happen, however, for very soon thereafter we approached the first of the big rapids. Abruptly, a great wave hit us. Our skipper maneuvered the barge expertly but our rafts twisted and twirled. Visibility downstream was obscured by mist and spray as we were swept into a chasm of churning foam.

We emerged drenched but smiling. We had not lost our humor. I was happy that I had not been washed overboard by the very first of the big rapids. The mounting board, tripod and camera had been torn loose but Ernst had kept the dragon from taking any of our equipment.

I still hear the roar of the river which made a constant deep-toned thunderous sound, its echo increased by the sheer cliffs. And I dream that I am riding the fury of Lava Falls, the most treacherous of the rapids, for it was here that a huge, hissing wave hit us, and it seemed as if the enormous power of the water would tear our rafts apart. Huge lateral waves broke over our barge in quick succession. The ropes creaked and groaned. I was in the middle raft riding high on a twenty foot wave when I saw Ernst (who was in the lead raft with the camera) go down in what seemed to be an enormous pit. I watched him disappear behind great dark boulders submerged in the river. A cavern of water poured over him in angry whirlpools

229 and I lost sight. I wondered what was happening. Was he over-

board? Then, my raft started going down into the pit. Before it could rise again, a breaker caught us and the third raft was catapulted on top of me. Another huge wave and the positions of the rafts were reversed. It was like a violent earthquake.

It was here at Lava Falls, 179 miles from Lees Ferry, approximately one million years ago, that a river of lava poured into the great gorge and dammed the Colorado. Through the centuries the river has eaten away the lava but the rapid remains the most treacherous of all the rapids on the voyage from Lees Ferry to Lake Mead.

Of course, there were moments of superb beauty. The solitude—a profound silence prevailed everywhere. The extraordinary opportunity to be completely isolated—the joy of seeing no automobiles and hearing no telephones. In a narrow inner gorge Dan pointed out to us some of the oldest rocks known to man. Also, spectacular Redwall limestone, with formations ranging from approximately 450 to 550 feet in thickness, ancient Indian cliff dwellings, a beautiful "castle" formation which proved that nature is the best architect of all.

The wildflowers were ablaze with color. The mallow plant, princess plume and the tamarisk bloomed profusely in full dress as if they were completely unaware that there was seldom anyone around to admire their beauty. There were heaps of ocotillo, barrel and hedgehog cacti and narrowleaf yucca as well as various kinds of lizards and small desert animals. The changes in plant and animal life encountered from the high altitude of the rim to the bottom of the Grand Canyon are comparable to those found between southern Canada and the deserts of Mexico. It was very hot and sultry usually averaging twenty degrees warmer at the bottom of the Canyon than on the rims. The life jackets which our skipper insisted

that we wear at all times, even in a smooth-flowing current, made us still more uncomfortable. Sometimes there were sudden showers during which the rain fell in torrents. In between showers the sun came out so the river was like a vast steam bath. But, after the storm was over, with the sun spreading its gold, the Canyon was like newborn. It was miraculously beautiful with colors ranging from orange to vermilion and a deep purple.

Many books have been written about the Colorado River but perhaps no one really knows it until he has had the opportunity to "shoot the rapids" after which he has earned the title of "River Rat". The Colorado has become known by its unchanging muddy color. The Mexicans call it the Rio Colorado—the great Red River of the West. It carries past any given point an average of nearly a half million tons of suspended silt every 24 hours. It begins in the high Rockies of Colorado and ends in the Gulf of California. It is approximately 2000 miles long—the second longest river in the United States. The Colorado averages about 300 feet in width, varies from 12 to 45 feet in depth, and flows at a speed of 2½ to 12½ miles per hour. It can be lazy and gentle one day and every "River Rat" will tell you, a roaring monster the next.

We drifted out on the clear waters of Lake Mead just eighteen days after the start of our run. There was a momentary feeling of elation, but, ironically, even before we reached Las Vegas, we all longed to be back on the River again—to hear her deep, deafening roar—to ride one of the high waves!

Upon our return to the South Rim, the summer heat was in full force. Tourists arrived from all over the world, particularly every corner of the United States. The visitors came and went. Mostly, they remained only one night. The menu at the restaurant was always the same as it was geared for such guests. "It is easier to change the guests than the menu", Ernst chuckled. In spite of the lack of variety, we had enormous appetites and felt extremely well. The 6,900 ft. altitude of the South Rim agreed with us. We supplemented our diet by purchasing fresh fruit from the market. Every day we continued our watch until the heat and glaze of the sun gave way to the coolness of the night.

The astonishing thing about the Grand Canyon is its variety, its capacity to be ever-changing in mood and color. It is literally alive with moods. Watching from the South Rim in the morning, when the light slants lengthwise from the Painted Desert, one sees the great capes of the opposite rim suddenly outlined in golden light, against which their shapes loom in hazy blues. Down in the gorge, here and there, streches of the Colorado River reflect the sunlight.

An hour later all is changed. The dark capes are brilliant-hued and well defined. Scores of new temples have emerged from the purple gloom. At midday the opposite walls have flattened and the capes and temples have lost their definite shadows. But as the afternoon wears on, the spectacles of the morning creep back, now reversed and strangely altered in outline.

We spent several days filming the proud and eccentric roadrunner which surely must be one of the most comical birds in the world. He has a speckled coat, a brilliantly colored head, short wings and a sharp bill. Add to this, a long neck, longer legs and an even longer tail. He has four toes, two pointing forward and two pointing backward and he leaves a curious track in the sand. He is noted for running at great speed, an estimated 15 miles per hour.

The roadrunner is a native bird of North America, ranging from Texas through New Mexico, Arizona, Kansas, Oklahoma, Colorado, California and most of Mexico. The Mexicans call it paisano. The word means "countryman". Others prefer the name faisen (pheasant), although the bird belongs to the cuckoo family. There is much folklore concerning the roadrunner. It appears in the legends of many of the Indian tribes. It is usually considered to be a sacred bird and most Indians believe that its presence is a sign of good luck. The roadrunner is extraordinarily proficient at killing the rattlesnake.

Filming the roadrunner was a fascinating experience. He was full of curiosity about everything and constantly entertained us with his comical antics. He would dart down a path, suddenly stop, stand dead still for a moment, cock his head from side to side, then streak out again. He appeared to have very keen eyesight, spotting insects at a remarkable distance. If he could find some sand, he wallowed in it and lost himself in the ecstasies of a dust bath. He seemed to enjoy the hot sun and seldom sought refuge in the shadows. He made a fascinating sound, rolling and trilling with his vocal organs. "Our roadrunner is a glutton", Ernst sighed dejectedly. We waited patiently while he ran around for two hours with an enormous lizard, half as long as he, dangling out of his mouth. According to the experts, after he has got a certain portion of it down, he must wait for the digestive juices to act before he can swallow further. In addition to his voracious appetite for lizards, he loved tarantulas, scorpions, horned toads and bumble bees.

At the end of July or August the thunderstorms were due to pass over the Canyon. As we wanted to match the *Cloudburst* movement of the music, we put up our camera on a special spot and started to wait. Each morning we set up all of the equipment. The sun beat down on us. Our bodies dripped with perspiration. We waited on, speechless. Days passed and still no rain fell. We watched the sky which was empty and barren. From dawn to dawn there was not a single cloud. At night the stars hung bright from the sky.

Finally, a few small clouds started to gather unwillingly in the sky. The wind began to blow. Ernst observed the clouds and said:

"There will be no rain today, but tomorrow perhaps, if the wind continues." The wind blew stronger and stronger. It started ripping the leaves from the trees. Encircling black clouds made the expanse of the Canyon seem to be boundless. A butterfly fluttered in the wind with torn wings, trying to fly away from the approaching storm. A raven, circling over the Canyon, plummeted downward, as its wings appeared to suddenly slip in the air. Clouds moved in from the direction of Death Valley. It got darker and darker. It was like the slow moving of an avalanche. The air was thick and heavy and an atmosphere of suspense hung over the Canyon. It was difficult to breathe. Then, we saw the first streak of lightning. And, the awesome effect of nature's magnitude engulfed us as it thundered in the distance. We felt the first drop of rain. The storm was upon us. There was a sudden and violent downpour, interspersed with the crashing thunder and lightning. Then, a virtual cloudburst. The persistent drive of the rain, the lightning, the thunder, all combined to produce a terrifying effect.—Suddenly, it was all over. The storm over the Grand Canyon disappeared as rapidly as a storm in the desert. In an instant the sun came out from behind the clouds.

Ernst is gifted with a pragmatic single-mindedness and insists in remaining on a spot when it would seem quite pointless to anyone else. The storm was over but it had left me a little terrified. I was eager to return to the security of the hotel for warm and dry clothing. He stood resolutely until a magnificent rainbow encircled the Canyon from the top ridges deep down in the gorge. He also has an uncanny sense of something about to happen and he usually knows long ahead (like the animals) when the weather is going to

234

change. We thought that we would never tire of looking at the autumn leaves, of watching the squirrels storing up nuts for their winter sleep. They were so busy we felt that they had only a few days left.

In September we moved over to the North Rim of the Grand Canyon for filming the deer. The animals are much more abundant there than on the South Rim and we preferred to search them out in the wilds for it smelled of adventure. "If we want to join them, we will have to know all about them", Ernst said. "We must learn their habits—their secret meeting places and grazing grounds—their favorite waterholes."

The North Rim is 8,100 feet in altitude, 1200 feet higher than the South Rim. Consequently, one looks down upon the vast temples which form the background of the panorama from the opposite rim. While the long series of buttes limit the view from Bright Angel Point to the east and west, from the North Rim one experiences a closeness to the Canyon that does not exist elsewhere. Gazing far into the distance, many miles beyond the South Rim, one sees the blue San Francisco Peaks towering some 6,000 feet above the level tableland.

The North Rim also includes a part of one of America's most beautiful forests, the Kaibab, with dense virgin stands of pine, fir, spruce and aspen. Because of the forecast for an unusually early snowfall, the lodge had already closed for the winter. However, an unused ranger's hut located at the edge of the forest was made available to us. And, if we were lucky, and quiet as a mouse, we could sometimes observe deer, squirrels, skunks and wild turkeys right in our own backyard. We shall never forget the fragile beauty of the yellow-dressed aspens in the early morning and late afternoon light. When the great ball of fire had finally descended, however, there was sudden and complete darkness. It was awesome. The old expression, "you can't see your hand before you", was literally true. As everything was abandoned, there were no lights in the vicinity except the tiny glow from our kerosene lamp. Sometimes, of course, there was the light of the moon which sparkled glints of silver over the silhouetted aspens.

Even though the days were quite pleasantly warm, the temperature dropped abruptly at nightfall, and we nearly froze in our little hut. We seldom saw anyone as warnings had been issued that snow was expected and it is possible for the roads to become blocked overnight.

Our plans were worked out in close detail. Mornings were spent searching out likely locations of the deer. Meals, etc., all fitted into a rigid pattern requiring a minimum of time. Late afternoons, when the deer first started to emerge from the forest, found us always near a waterhole or grazing ground with our camera ready for action. The sight of the first deer was always exciting. They usually stood silently at the edge of the forest (hidden amongst patches of shade and sunlight) then ventured out with a marvelous grace and suppleness of movement.

The animals started gathering around four o'clock. The old bucks usually led the herd. The females and young followed. When fawns were in the group, the adults almost always kept them screened with their own bodies. There was generally an air of watchfulness amongst the animals and one of them—usually an old buck—appeared to stand guard. Despite the fact that he nibbled peacefully, his ears were always on the alert. And, if he sensed danger, for some reason or another, he made an immense leap, and the entire herd bounded back into the forest like a group of ballet dancers.

The cause of the alarm was usually too subtle for us to discern. But, once or twice it appeared to be a warning flight of birds. The bright

alert eyes turned out to be very weak. But the animals very quickly became aware of our presence through their acute senses of smelling and hearing. We were extremely cautious to remain downwind, crushing clods of earth into sand to determine the direction of the breeze. Still, a sudden gust seemed always to expose us. Fewer and fewer deer grazed in the grasslands or drank from the waterhole—for the air smelled of man.

Of all the animals in the Grand Canyon National Park (which includes 180 species of birds, 60 species of mammals, 25 reptiles and 5 amphibians) we had most wanted to become friends with the deer. We had hoped to run with them—to share their play and their silences. We had approached their benign world with a great deal of caution. But, they refused to accept us. They sniffed the air reproachfully. Man was clearly their enemy.

We took long walks through the magnificent Kaibab Forest. The light laughed through the majestic aspen, pine and spruce. Resting at ease on a bough of a tree, we spotted a white-tailed Kaibab squirrel which is found nowhere else in the world. He looked freshly scrubbed and brushed.—Occasionally we came too close to a yellow-haired porcupine and he bristled with rage. His quills and antenna-like guard hairs stood on end as if charged with electricity. We laughed at him but tried to keep our distance, for porky is formidably armed with an estimated 30,000 quills which are constantly replaced when lost in combat.—From a low-slung branch, a beautiful bird twittered, then filled the air with her song. She did not know we listened. We tiptoed closer, but she was off at once on her luxurious wings. We lingered awhile and watched the red and golden flutterings.

The silence in the forest was so complete that even the fall of a single leaf seemed to make a loud thud. Giant dead trees lay still and quiet on the ground. It appeared that no one had disturbed them for at least a half a century. They were bone-white, in mysterious, abstract forms—strangely beautiful. Some had almost deteriorated—gone back to the earth from whence they had come.

Northwest of the Grand Canyon National Park is the Grand Canyon National Monument which comprises 314 square miles. It includes Toroweap Point and affords a remarkable view of the Colorado River locked in sheer depths of over 2,900 feet. It was in this remote and dramatically beautiful location that we filmed most of the animals: mountain lions, skunks, coyotes, and bobcats. There were many superb features—precipitous, dark, rugged overhanging ledges; numerous pinnacles and towers in a great variety of forms. We were surrounded by great cliffs and steep slopes.

From this advantageous sight one had a perfect view of the rushing, turbulent water of the Colorado River and the steep dark walls far down below. In the distance, behind the ridges and temples, rose the volcanic peaks of Mount Trumbull—remnants of craters which often in times past poured out streams of lava. The whole area was packed with beauty and charm and adventure.

Winter came suddenly to the Grand Canyon. There was an awesome silence and in the morning the Canyon lay white. The pines, under a coating of snow, rose sheer from the white ground to the sky. The white of the snow made the deep gorge deeper still. The temples and buttes took on new forms. We stood long hours in the cold loneliness with our faces buried in mufflers. American air force boots (with thick sheepskin lining) covered our feet. Still, we were purple from the cold as we patiently time-lapsed the battles of the black and white clouds, ice freezing, then breaking up into artistic patterns, melting and freezing again. We filmed the trees and shrubs covered with piles of snow, enormous icicles hanging from the
238 Canyon walls.

A tender dandelion forcing its way through the frozen earth was the first indication that spring was again at hand. The four seasons had been completed—a year's work accomplished—the long wait had finally ended. I was suddenly reminded of a passage I had read in the diary of Major John Wesley Powell (the first man to explore the Colorado River and its unmapped canyons) which was written in 1869: "You cannot see the Grand Canyon in one view... but if strength and courage are sufficient for the task, by a year's toil a concept of sublimity can be obtained never again to be equaled on the hither side of Paradise."

The day was over and cries of wildlife haunted the air of the slowly dying light over the Canyon. The sky seemed to be on fire. Then, the glowing ball that was the sun sank gradually into the wondrous shades of purple, orange and deep crimson. It was in this atmosphere that we last saw the Grand Canyon before returning to our home in Hollywood. One more glance—far, far above the threading Colorado River an eagle seemed to float and carry us with him over the vast temples and buttes.

Jean Heiniger

Brief captions

129 Dead tree in autumnal grass
130 Aspen mingling with Colorado blue spruce
131 Interesting cloud formation
132 Approaching thunderstorm over the Grand Canyon.
    Kanab Point, North Rim
133 Lightning over the Grand Canyon
134 The storm passes
135 View from Desert View Point, South Rim
136 Snow-covered rock buttress
137 Grand Canyon after a snowfall
138 Canyon wall after a thunderstorm
139 Bright Angel Trail in the snow
140 View from snow-bound South Rim into the
    snowless canyon
141 Mysterious atmosphere in the wintery Grand Canyon
142 Melting ice cover with juniper twig
143 The Canyon after the first snow
144 Trees and shrubs covered with snow
145 Great horned owl on a snow-covered branch
146 Clump of grass and stones in the snow
147 Young cottontail rabbit
148 Snow-covered tree on the South Rim before the
    snowless Canyon
149 Melting snow on a red sand dune
150 Snow-covered shrub in canyon landscape
151 Dead tree trunk and clump of grass after a blizzard
152 Snow-covered tree in front of snowless buttes
    in the gorge
153 Confluence of the blue Little Colorado and the
    muddy Colorado River
154 Water-filled rock pools at the canyon rim
155 Rainbow over the Grand Canyon
156 Coyote on an overhanging rock slab
157 Sunset

133

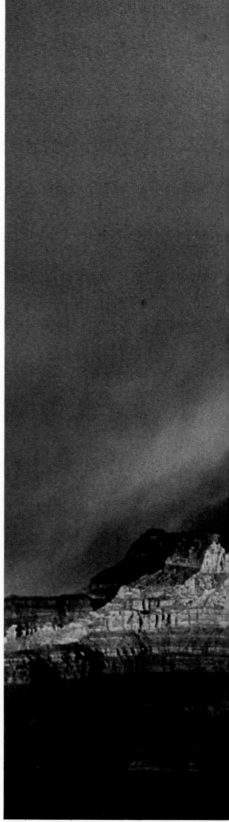

134

144

146

147

149

150

151

152

153

154

155

# Commentary on Pictures

1 Darkness recedes. Day breaks over the Grand Canyon: the cirrus clouds are already brilliantly lit while the lower cloud layers are just being touched by the sun's first rays.

2 Rock temples and buttes: a single moment in the constant change of color and atmosphere. Toward the late afternoon the shadows have hard outlines. View from the North Rim; from left to right: Boysag Point, Paya Point, Torwago Point. The Grand Canyon is about 4 to 20 miles wide and 217 miles long. The most picturesque part is within the territory of the Grand Canyon National Park which covers an area of 1,100 square miles.

3 Navajo shepherds in the lonely Monument Valley with its red sandstone buttes and its almost polished rock needles and pillars which tower more than 300 feet above the valley floor.

4 Monument Valley, belonging to the area of the Navajo Reservation, is the quintessence of the immense wide open spaces typical of the west of the United States. The valley is famous for its exotic colors which appear different in different weather. Extreme temperatures and the wind have given a kind of polish to the rock surfaces.

5 About noon the profile of the rock faces opposite appears to have flattened and projections and rock temples have lost their well-defined shadows. The shadows cast by the cumulus clouds, which are typical of the summer weather, enliven the canyon with additional atmospheric touches.

6 Navajo shepherds driving their flock over the red sand in search of grazing. The typical patterning of the sand dunes, called ripple marks, has been produced by the wind.

7 A handsome Navajo shepherd. The Navajos are semi-nomads who meet a large part of their subsistence by sheep-keeping. These animals as a rule are the property of the women since most Navajos still live in a matriarchal society. Horses and cattle, on the other hand, are traditionally the property of the men.

8 Lonely track in the vast magnificent Monument Valley. Here one feels the heroic grandeur of the Wild West. The location shots for many a famous film, including "Stagecoach", were made in this valley.

9 The craft of weaving is one of the most important sources of revenue of the Navajos. It is said that each carpet is an individual creation of the woman weaver. The Navajos prefer bold simple patterns.

10 "Montezuma Castle" is one of the best-preserved Indian rock dwellings; it probably dates from between the tenth and twelfth centuries. It is about 33 feet high and 72 feet wide. The overhanging rock made a surprise attack from above impossible and the occupants were able to spot an approaching enemy a long way off.

11 The Painted Desert, discovered in the 16th century by the Spaniards who named it "Desierto Pintado", is a desert-like dissected landscape with fantastically colored buttes, and plateaus with deep incisions. The interesting erosion shapes are due to rain.

12/13 Detailed photographs of Plate 11, showing the effect of precipitation and water running down the slope. They produce the interesting erosion "sculptures". The loose material is washed away while sharp-edged rock fragments collect in the gullies and large blocks occasionally remain poised for a long time on top of earth pillars which thus are themselves protected by their boulder caps.

14 "The Big Eye", another impressive example of nature in a playfully creative mood in Monument Valley. Rock arches of this kind also exist in the Alps.

15 Spider Rock, an 804-foot obelisk, at the spot where Monument Canyon and Canyon de Chelly unite. This is Indian country. The present-day Navajos build their summer huts—the typical earth-covered block houses called "hogans"—in the valleys in order to cultivate their crops and watch their sheep.

16 This petrified tree trunk in the Petrified National Forest looks as if it had only just crashed to the ground—a silent witness to the changes to which climate and vegetation are subject.

17 Detail of a petrified tree trunk in the Petrified Forest. These trees flourished some 160 million years ago; the predominant species resembled the pine nowadays native to Arizona.

18 Gravel mingled with chips and fragments of petrified tree trunks forms the brilliantly colorful ground cover of the Petrified Forest. The fragments sometimes still reveal the organic structure (annual rings) of the stems.

19 Strikingly colored splinters of petrified wood. The color patterns are due to the action of iron and manganese oxide; the predominant type of these hues is known as agate.

20 The tumbleweed *Salsola iberica* in the Painted Desert. Here we see another type of erosion shape (see Plate 13)—the boulders seem as if piled on top of each other by giant hands.

21 This yucca, or Spanish bayonet *(Yucca harrimaniae)* has a half-shrivelled look. But appearances are deceptive: it has a remarkable power of survival. With its narrow sword-like leaves it resembles an African aloe.

22 A dead giant pine. Resembling bleached bone, this truncated branch suggests the strangely bizarre skull of a dinosaur. The weathering process often creates the most fantastic shapes.

23 The knothole of the dead pine no longer tempts a bird to nest in it. Forbidding and rigid it seems to belong to a world which is no longer life and not yet quite death.

24 Decomposition has largely reduced this tree trunk *(Pinus edulis)* and in the process revealed its basic geometric structure. Like life and death, the organic and the abstract closely resemble each other in this strange landscape, testifying to their mysterious identity.

25 Giant cactus or saguaro *(Carnegiea gigantea)* near Tucson. This species with its candelabra-like branches often possesses a severe symmetrical beauty. This specimen is interesting by its very irregularity.

26 Flowering saguaro *(Carnegiea gigantea):* its blossom together with the cactus wren is the emblem of the state of Arizona. The fruit is regarded as a great delicacy by the Indians.

27 Desert View Observation Tower is a modern reconstruction of the towers built by the Indians centuries ago. Made of local stone, it also provides unique views of the Grand Canyon and the Painted Desert.

28 The shadow play of drifting clouds enlivens the rigid grandeur of rock faces and buttes. View from the northern part of Havasu Canyon. From left to right: Boysag Point, Shanub Point.

29 Pinyon pine *(Pinus edulis)* on the South Rim of the Grand Canyon. Its shape, formed in battle against the elements, is more picturesque in its idiosyncrasy than that of more regular trees in sheltered positions.

30 View from Bright Angel Point on the North Rim. The light of the setting sun strikes the canyon; the buttresses of the opposite rim are veiled in blue mist while the rock temples in the foreground suddenly appear as if steeped in gold. From left to right: Brahma Temple, Zoroaster Temple.

31 Kanab Canyon with Kanab Creek in the foreground, seen from Kanab Point on the North Rim. This is almost a demonstration model of erosion at work in a canyon: the topographical forms resulting from stratification on the one hand and dissection of the sedimentary rock on the other can be clearly seen.

32 View from Yaki Point down the precipice of the Grand Canyon. The stratified formations in the upper part of the canyon are clearly distinguished from the crystalline bedrock of the Inner Gorge.

33 The Colorado seen from Toroweap Point in the Grand Canyon National Monument. This spot provides a particularly good view of the river and the dark precipitous rock faces. The river rises in the Colorado Rockies and runs into the Gulf of California on Mexican territory. With a length of 1,988 miles it is the second longest river of the United States. Its average width is 295 feet, its depth 13 to 46 feet and its rate of flow 2½ to 12 miles per hour. During each 24 hours it carries 500,000 tons of mud, no matter where the measurement is made.

34 Rock overhang on the Kaibab Trail on the South Rim—the result of differential weathering. The golden brown of the rock makes a fine contrast with the purple of the buttes and rock faces in the background.

35 View of the Colorado from the trail leading down to Lava Falls—a name that goes back to Major John Wesley Powell. Here, at Lava Falls, 178 miles from Lees Ferry, a stream of lava poured into the ravine about a million years ago and blocked the flow of the Colorado. In his diary Major Powell noted: "What a conflict of water and fire there must have been here!"

36 The boats on which we drifted down the Colorado from Lees Ferry, Arizona, to Lake Mead, California; each of them weighed 13 tons. We covered a distance of 235 miles. The three boats were lashed together with nylon ropes; thus abreast they had an area of about 21 by 28 feet. Our camera equipment, clothes, sleeping bags and food supplies for 18 days had to be stowed in waterproof bags and these, for reasons of safety, were secured with ropes bound at the top of our raft.

37 Jean Heiniger on the raft. We all had kapok-padded life jackets and we were made to wear them even when running through calm water.

38/40 One of our main problems was driftwood which caused us a good deal of trouble especially toward the end of our voyage in the area of Lake Mead.

39 Ernie Shultz, our botanist, who identified the plants along the river banks.

41 Ernst A. Heiniger, getting his film camera ready for a new sequence.

42 Park Ranger Dan Davis and our botanist Ernie Shultz about to secure the raft to the beach.

43 Parched bank of the Colorado. The rust-colored mud develops bizzare cracks and fissures under the scorching sun.

44 Tamarisks *(Tamarix pentandra)* on the edge of the bank. Its flowers provide pale pink patches in the dead monotony of the gorge (see Plate 52).

45 The abandoned raft riding on the Colorado. We usually climbed up some high rock to eat our food or pitch camp.

46 The waves of the Colorado are wild, tempestuous and incalculable. The muddy tint which has given the river its name further heightens the sense of elemental menace.

47 The Mexicans called the river "Rio Colorado", the American pioneers mostly "Great Red River of the West"—both because of the reddish color of the water. From one day to the next its mood may abruptly change: it can act like a roaring monster and then again flow along peacefully and lethargically as in this picture.

48 Willow about to unfold its leaves on the bank of the Colorado.

49 The canyon walls are not equally resistant to erosion everywhere; this results in the most varied types of terrace, scarp and plinth formation. The rock niche in the picture is such a product of erosion. The water occasionally dripping from the overhanging rock has created an oasis of vegetation in the rocky desert.

50 Large cave-like alcove hollowed out over the centuries by wind and rain. Here too there are traces of vegetation on the lower lip.

51 *Yucca elata* on the bank of the Colorado. Along with the cacti the yuccas are the "exotic" plants of this region—in the colloquial rather than the strictly scientific meaning of the word.

52 Flowering tamarisk *(Tamarix pentandra)*. The delicate flowers and leaves make a striking contrast to the monumental rigidity and grandeur of the canyon.

53 Overhang in the Toroweap area on the North Rim of the Grand Canyon. These are typical biotopes of the lichen *Acarospora* which withdraws lime from the substratum and secretes it on its surface.

54 Time and again one encounters perfect "architectural" forms such as this castle-like structure on the walls of the Grand Canyon—further proof that nature is the greatest architect.

55 These impressively weathered horizontal rock strata were originally deposits of sand, mud and lime in a prehistoric sea. The thick stratum in the middle reveals so-called cross-bedding as found in sand dunes nowadays.

56 As a rule the sedimentary deposits are horizontal—but there are irregularities. This picture from the lower part of the canyon shows a marked folding of sedimentary strata.

57 In the area of the Grand Canyon there are very few water courses running into the Colorado. One of these is shown in the picture: it reaches the river as a small but vigorous waterfall which has cut a chimney-type cleft into the canyon's rock wall.

58 Detail of the Toroweap lava flow, showing the "pillow" structure of the rock formation, a form of weathering typical of columnar basalt.

59 An ocotillo shrub *(Fouquieria splendens):* its Spanish name has been taken over by the Americans. Its excessively thin twigs give it a pronouncedly bizarre appearance.

60 Only a few feet above the low water level of the Colorado the rock face shows the typical marks of erosion and "polishing" caused by the river in spate.

61 The wind raises the sand and blows it across the canyon. There it collects and trickles down the scarp of the river bank.

62 Sand banks which have come into being along the river bed of the Colorado are eroded as the river cuts through its own deposits. This erosion is doubly effective when the sand bank is also undercut in the river bends.

63 Ocotillo *(Fouquieria splendens)* on the bank of the Colorado. The red blossoms heighten the exotic charm of this plant (see Plate 59).

64 Close-up of two inflorescences of the ocotillo *(Fouquieria splendens).* This shows clearly the arrangement of leaves typical of this plant.

65 Sandstone cliffs with rock-mat *(Petrophyton caespitosum).* This is a close relation of *Spiraea.*

66 A typical river bank still-life with cacti and mallows *(Sphaeralcea sp.).* The change in vegetation from the upper rim down to the floor of the canyon is analogous to that experienced when one crosses the landscapes between Southern Canada and the Mexican deserts.

67 The mallow *(Sphaeralcea sp.)* flowers with positive tropical splendor on the river bank at the bottom of the canyon—pointlessly, it might seem, since human beings only rarely get near enough to admire its beauty.

68 Common sotol *(Dasylirion wheeleri)* and ocotillo *(Fouquieria splendens)* among the rocks close to the river bank. The inclination of the sedimentary strata is quite striking (see Plate 56).

69 Elves Chasm, where Royal Arch Creek empties into the river in an entrancing waterfall. We were delighted with the lush vegetation and the crystal clearness of the water.

70/71 Elves Chasm again—this gorge was one of the most wonderful impressions of our voyage down the Colorado. Here the colors of the canyon seem to have a particularly intensive brilliance.

72 Old man prickly pear *(Opuntia erinacea).* The sharp spines on the joints do not detract from the beauty of this plant. The picture shows a specimen whose magnificent blossoms are about to open.

73 Hedgehog cactus *(Echinocereus engelmannii).* The longitudinal ribs of the stem are lined with humps and are usually studded with spines. The beauty of cactus flowers never ceases to surprise the beholder.

74 A grizzly bear cactus *(Opuntia erinacea ursina,* on the right) and barrel cacti *(Ferocactus acanthodes).* Not only the color of the flowers but also that of the stem varies from one cactus species to another.

75 *Opuntia violacea.* Even within the same genus *(Opuntia)* there are the most interesting variations of color (see Plate 72).

76 Barrel cactus *(Ferocactus acanthodes),* a magnificent solitary specimen of the species shown in Plate 74 (to the left).

77 Buckhorn cholla *(Opuntia acanthocarpa).* Like its relative *Opuntia erinacea* it produces spectacular yellow blossoms (see Plate 72).

78 A beautiful small forest lake on the North Rim of the canyon under the autumn sun which gilds the marsh grass and aspen leaves *(Populus tremuloides).*

79 The coyote *(Canis latrans),* an intelligent and adaptable small wolf, comes to terms with any biotope within its vast area of distribution—even the rocky ravines of the canyon.

80 The mule-deer *(Odocoileus hemionus)* is represented in Arizona by special subspecies. Only exceptionally will it leave its lush feeding grounds in forests and clearings to venture into the jagged rocky terrain. The picture shows the Kaibab Forest; in the background, *Picea pungens* and *Populus tremuloides.*

81 The urson *(Erethizon dorsatum)* is also known as a tree porcupine. It is in fact a true rodent and one of the largest. Here a yellow specimen displays the halo of its erectile spine-studded bristly fur.

82 When the relatively long tail of the mule-deer, which belongs to the tailed deer, is not visible, the animal resembles the European roe.

83 Unlike the European red deer the mule-deer, which occurs in many different subspecies, does not live in large herds but usually—as in this picture—in small groups.

84 As in its nearest relative, the white-tailed deer *(Odocoileus virginianus),* the ears of the mule-deer are powerfully developed and rotatable in all directions. This is to ensure the earliest possible discovery of an enemy.

85 Without any doubt the most impressive bird of prey of the Grand Canyon is the golden eagle. All mammals, even fawns and mountain lion cubs, have to be on guard against it.

86 A young mountain lion *(Puma concolor)* moving noiselessly through a typical canyon landscape. The fully grown animal can be a threat to deer and even to the urson.

87 Like the coyote among the canine predators, the bobcat *(Lynx rufus)* among the feline predators is an exceedingly adaptable species, readily at home in all biotopes. Occasionally the hair tufts on the ears, normally typical of lynxes, are absent.

88 Three adolescent mountain lions, which have already lost the spotted fur of the young animal, are fascinated by some stimulus on the right—possibly the photographer's assistant. The two nearer animals clearly show the so-called ear pouches, a doubling of the outer ear whose significance is still a mystery to zoologists.

89 It does not take much to trigger off a defensive expression on the mountain lion's features. The whiskers, normally lying against the skin, are directed forward and the nose is turned up.

90 This picture shows with particular clarity that the mule-deer belongs to the tailed deer.

91 The golden eagle *(Aquila chrysaëtos)*—the proud heraldic beast of the U.S.A.—was forced, like its European relative, to forsake most of its original area of distribution and to withdraw to less densely populated regions.

92 The rocky setting of this picture explains why the puma is known in America as the mountain lion—even though these are not high towering mountains but the deep ravines of the Grand Canyon.

93 Along with the spotted jaguar—the "tiger" of the New World—the mountain lion or puma is the biggest predatory cat of America.

94 A young mountain lion whose skin still shows traces of the juvenile spotted fur among the fissured rocks of the Grand Canyon.

95 A spotted skunk *(Spilogale putorius)* huddling in a small rock cave, seeking cover. Unlike his relative, the skunk proper, it is a skilled climber who has been found in tree hollows over 30 feet above the ground.

96 The cacomistle *(Bassariscus astutus)* with its beautifully ringed tail is rarely seen in European zoos. Even in its natural home—which includes the Grand Canyon—its extremely shy behavior means that it is only infrequently sighted by humans.

97 The needle-shaped spines of *Opuntia fulgida* do not stop the mourning dove *(Zenaidura macroura)* from building its simple nest on it. Indeed it has a preference for these cacti which provide effective protection against various enemies on the ground.

98 The ears of this soaked bobcat show—or at least suggest—the fine hair tufts which are typical of all

lynxes in the Old and New World in addition to their short tails.

99 The splendid view of the Colorado River in its deep gorge evidently impresses these young mountain lions a lot less than it does the tourists from all over the world.

100 The small traces of snow in the shaded cracks of the weathered wood suggest that the mountain lion is stretching lazily in the spring sunshine. Or is this—as it is with other cats—a sign that its mating season has begun?

101 This close-up shows the roadrunner *(Geococcyx californianus)*, the most popular bird of North America. This cuckoo, which has a wide distribution area, enjoys universal popularity largely because it is an eager killer of snakes and also takes its toll of scorpions, spiders and other venomous creatures.

102–117 This series of shots offers another reason for the busy roadrunner's general popularity: it is almost continually in motion throughout the day and many of its attitudes are downright comical—from its tufted feathered crest to its erectile tail, from the litheness of its head and the play of its beak to its tripping gait. It is hardly ever seen in flight. To encounter one of these amusing roadrunners is considered lucky.

118 Young bobcat *(Lynx rufus),* evidently taken by surprise and cornered on this projecting boulder. Its face and raised paw suggest extreme alertness for defense.

119 This mountain lion appears to have been disturbed during its siesta: its ears are slightly folded back, its whiskers a little agitated—but so far it sees no reason for getting up. Evidently the photographer has come near to crossing the animal's escape distance.

120 The gray fox *(Urocyon cinereoargentatus)* with its attractive golden-red collar enjoying a well camouflaged rest in the half-shade.

121 The sidewinder *(Crotalus cerastes)* is a very venomous representative of the rattlesnakes and well adapted to life in the hot sand. Its name refers to its curious mode of locomotion.

122 The sidewinder is the only snake of the New World which leaves not a continuous track in the sand but one composed of separate "footsteps". It uses, roughly speaking, two sections of its body as if they were legs, raising and setting them down alternately.

123 The Gila monster *(Heloderma suspectum),* one of the only two venomous lizards, can grow to a length of about 20 inches. The tail of this desert lizard serves it for the storage of fat, somewhat like a camel's hump. The creature in the picture has largely consumed its store.

124 Large spiders resembling the bird spiders of South America are occasionally encountered in the Grand Canyon. They should not be touched because their bite can cause poisoning and the fine hairs can cause inflammation of mucous membranes.

125 Coyote (in the picture) and gray fox are often so similar in the landscape that from a distance they cannot easily be told apart. Both wild dog species can occur in the same territory, like the black-backed and the common jackal in East Africa.

126 The gray fox is very similar to the European fox and shares its predilection for small rodents and birds living on the ground.

127 The term "prairie wolf" is scarcely suitable now for the coyote in these eerie rocky ravines—but then this small wolf is capable of adapting itself to the most varied habitats.

128 The great horned owl *(Bubo virginianus)* is the biggest of the nocturnal birds of prey. Its quarry is much the same as that of the eagle, the biggest of diurnal birds of prey, yet the two predators are not rivals because their hunting hours are totally different.

129 Fallen dead tree in the autumnal grass. The broken branches, unlike the stem, are not yet entirely stripped of their bark.

130 Golden-leaved aspens mingled with Colorado blue spruce: the picture was taken on the edge of the Kaibab forest on the North Rim of the Grand Canyon. The Kaibab forest with its dense untouched stands of pine, fir, spruce and aspen is

one of the most beautiful forest regions of the United States.

131 Clouds dissolve and reform as the seasons change, providing an interesting counterpoint to the majestic tranquility of the great gorge.

132 A heavy oppressive atmosphere lies over the Grand Canyon as a storm approaches. The view is from Kanab Point on the North Rim of the gorge.

133 Thunderstorms, accompanied by gales, usually hit the canyon suddenly and unexpectedly. After a gigantic thunderclap flashes of lightning in rapid succession light up the dark walls of the gorge.

134 A storm over the Grand Canyon usually passes as quickly as in the desert. The battle between light and darkness has already been decided.

135 After the storm the clouds drift away; far below, the Colorado still reflects the grey light. Desert View Point, South Rim.

136 Snow-covered rock buttress in the canyon wall. The seemingly black color of the rock is due to a runnel making its way down to the river.

137 During the long winter months the Kaibab Plateau is covered with snow and not accessible to tourists. It is not unknown for the snow cover to extend to the Coconino Plateau and even into the Grand Canyon itself.

138 After a thunderstorm the canyon walls are steeped in a mysterious darkness—only the light of the grey clouds is reflected from the wet rock face.

139 The South Rim of the Grand Canyon after a snowfall, seen from Maricopa Point. The Inner Gorge may be explored by taking the Bright Angel Trail which—clearly visible in the picture—leads down to the Colorado.

140 View from the South Rim into the snowless depths of the canyon. As with vegetation, the Inner Gorge and the Rim above belong to fundamentally different climatic zones (see caption to Plate 66).

141 Mysterious twilight in the wintery Grand Canyon. The outlines of the great gorge occasionally suggest the mystical motifs of Chinese or Japanese landscape painting.

142 Nature frequently reveals itself as the greatest artist—provided we have the eyes to see it. The picture shows a juniper twig among the bizarre shapes of the melting ice cover—an infallible sign of approaching spring.

143 Winter has come quite suddenly to the Grand Canyon. An awe-inspiring silence lies over the land as, one morning, the canyon is all covered in white.

144 The white coating on the trees and shrubs makes the gorge seem even deeper than it really is. The glittering cover makes one forget that only a short time ago the trees were totally bare. In the foreground a cliff rose *(Cowania mexicana)*.

145 The great horned owl *(Bubo virginianus,* see Plate 128) on a snow-covered branch. The breeding period of this largest of all nocturnal birds of prey is 34 to 36 days. The tufts of feathers above the owl's eyes are sometimes described as "tufted ears". However, they have no connection with the ears proper.

146 The snow cover in the canyon area is not deep enough to iron out unevennesses of the ground such as clumps of grass and stones.

147 Young Audubon's cottontail *(Sylvilagus audubonii)* ducking under a tuft of grass in a hollow in the snow. This rabbit was named in honor of the great ornithologist Jean-Jacques Audubon.

148 There is deep winter at the rim while the lower regions of the canyon are enjoying a warmer season. Yaki Point, South Rim.

149 Melting snow on a red sand dune. The unevennesses in the sand—like those in the snow—are partly due to human footmarks and partly to erosion.

150 This white-veiled shrub (cliff rose, *Cowania mexicana*) and the vague dissolving outlines of the background again suggest a Far Eastern brush drawing.

151 A dead tree trunk and withered grass after a
    blizzard—a winter still-life that might inspire a
    Japansese *haiku* about transience but also about
    the perpetuity of all life.

152 This might almost be an alpine scene in Europe.
    The illusion is somewhat marred by the fact that
    the (seemingly) higher summits in the background
    are clear of snow. In the foreground a cliff rose
    *(Cowania mexicana)*.

153 Confluence of the Little Colorado and the Colorado
    River. No picture could demonstrate more clearly
    the enormous quantities of mud carried by the
    main river; the Little Colorado is seen to be
    brilliantly blue.

154 Water-filled rock pools near the upper rim of the
    gorge. Here too we have a fascinating change of
    colors: according to the incidence of light the
    water's surface shimmers green, gray or white.

155 The thunderstorm is over and a magnificent
    rainbow arches over ridges and butte tops, reach-
    ing deep down into the gorge.

156 Once more we encounter a young coyote on a
    rock overhang. Even in such places fat rodents and
    birds may have their nests in rock crevices and
    tangles of vegetation, making it worthwhile for the
    hungry wild dog to search these fissured rocks.

157 The day is done. Gradually the light dies. The
    glowing orb of the sun slowly sinks amidst
    wonderful hues ranging from gold to vermilion.
    Dusk enfolds the Grand Canyon.

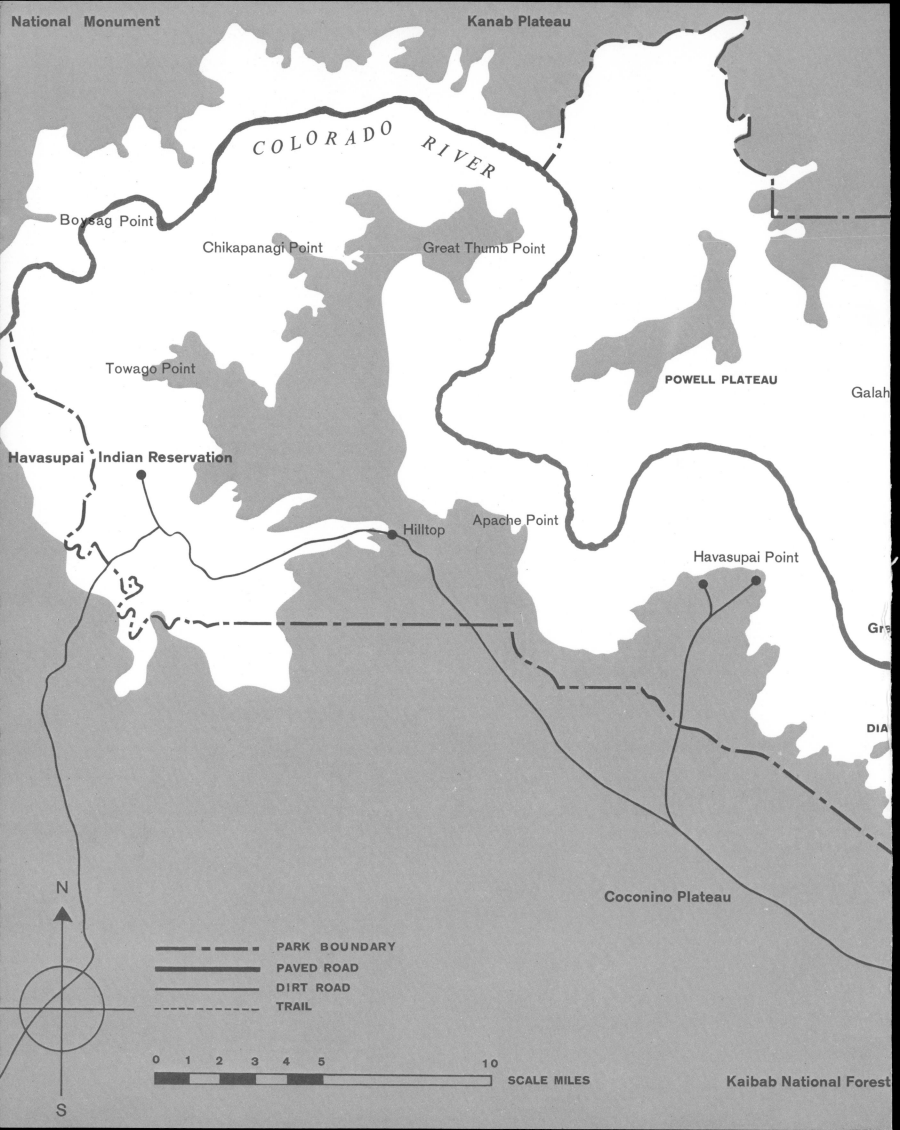